THE VISION OF LIFE 2

THE VISION OF LIFE 2

ELIYAHU KBABIEH

THE VISION OF LIFE 2

This book is written to provide information and motivation to readers. Its purpose is not to render any type of psychological, legal, or professional advice of any kind. The content is the sole opinion and expression of the author, and not necessarily that of the publisher.

Copyright © 2019 by Eliyahu Kbabieh

All rights reserved. No part of this book may be reproduced, transmitted, or distributed in any form by any means, including, but not limited to, recording, photocopying, or taking screenshots of parts of the book, without prior written permission from the author or the publisher. Brief quotations for noncommercial purposes, such as book reviews, permitted by Fair Use of the U.S. Copyright Law, are allowed without written permissions, as long as such quotations do not cause damage to the book's commercial value. For permissions, write to the publisher, whose address is stated below.

Printed in the United States of America.

ISBN   978-1-64552-051-1   (Paperback)
ISBN   978-1-64552-052-8   (Digital)

Lettra Press books may be ordered through booksellers or by contacting:

Lettra Press LLC
18229 E 52nd Ave.
Denver City, CO 80249
1 303 586 1431 | info@lettrapress.com
www.lettrapress.com

Dedicated in Honor of:

My dear wife, Bella Kbabieh

My parents, Yvette and Isaac Kbabieh

My in-laws, Shella and Moshe Yaich

Rabbi David Ashear *shlitah*

Rabbi Yaakov Kalmanowitz *shlitah*

This Book Has Been Sponsored by:

Emma & Sammy Faineh

Shlomo Faineh

Rabbi Ariel Mizrachi
in honor of his wife, Frida

Dr. Raymond Sultan
in honor of his wife, Hodaya

Joey Mamrout & Family Ouni Mamrout & Family

Chaim Malach & Family

This Book Has Been Sponsored By:

Yaakov Aghai

Henry Kameo & Family

The Sadaka Family

The Jajati Family

Albert Hanano & Family

Moshe Lati & Family

This Book Has Been Sponsored by:

Jimmy Malach in honor of his wife

Raquel Cohen & Family

Simon Salameh in honor of his wife

David Eliyahu & Family

Anonymous

Anonymous

Daily & Gary Blum

Shirley & Yossi Zafrani

In Memory of:

Yosef ben Miraim

Mazal bat Leah

Salim ben Rosa

Hassiba bat Miraim

Ezra ben Rachel

Ines bat Badiah

Salim ben Rosa
by Leila and David Saltz

Salim ben Rosa
by Shella and Moshe Yaich

Reruah Shelewa:

Yaakov Mordechai ben Malkah

Ovadia ben Ester

Avraham Moshe ben Rina

All of Klal Yisrael

STELLA LINIADO A"H
"A PURE SOUL TAKEN TOO SOON"

OUR BEAUTIFUL STELLA,
YOU HAVE LEFT US WAY TOO SOON FOR WORDS.
IN YOUR SHORT TIME HERE YOU HAVE SHOWN US STRENGTH WHEN WE WERE WEAK.
AND YOU GAVE US HAPPINESS TO KEEP US AFLOAT.
ALTHOUGH THERE ARE NO FOOTPRINTS FOR US TO FOLLOW, WE KNOW YOU WILL CARRY US ON THIS JOURNEY AND GUIDE US THROUGH OUR LIVES.
YOUR FULL OF LIFE SPIRIT AND ANGELIC BEAUTY IS OUR INSPIRATION TO KEEP MOVING FORWARD AND MAKE YOU PROUD.
YOU ARE AN EXAMPLE OF WHAT A DAUGHTER IS.
ONE OF A KIND!
OUR HEARTS BEAT DIFFERENTLY NOW.
YOU, OUR BEAUTIFUL STELLA ARE MISSED EVERY DAY!
WITH ALL OUR LOVE,
MOMMY, DADDY, MARC, JUSTIN, MICHAEL, AND SITTO.

BIRKAT YAAKOV
In Memory of Jack Adjmi ה"ע

Rabbi David Ozeri
Rabbi David Sutton

בס"ד

November, 2016

Eli Kbabieh is a very well meaning Ben Torah who inspires himself and others .
I did not have the chance to read this book in its entirety , but the little that I looked at was very uplifting.
I am sure that his good intentions and good heart will help others grow in Torah and Mitzvot.

Sincerely
Rabbi David Sutton

1032 Ocean Parkway • Brooklyn, NY 11230
Tel - (718) 677-3707 • Fax - (718) 677-3706

Darchei Noam Torah Center
1848 East 7th Street
Brooklyn, NY 11223
darcheinoam1@gmail.com

It gives me great pleasure to congratulate Mr, Eliyahu Kbabieh on the republishing of his book the "Vision of Life." Although I have not had the chance to read the book, I am confident that the reader will find it informative and inspiring as Eliyahu is a true Ben Torah who takes his learning and Avodat Hashem very seriously and is eager to constantly grow higher in levels of mussar and self-perfection. I wish him Hatzlacha in everything he does, and he should go mechayil el chayil!

Sincerely
Rabbi Mrad Sardar

דברי ברכה

יום ג' לסדר "ריח נחוח"
לה"' תשע"ט

לכבוד ידידי היקר ר' אליהו קבאביה שליט"א. ראו ראיתי מעט מלקט דברי המוסר שכת"ר העלה על הכתב. הנני בא לחזק את ידך "שחפץ ה' בידו יצלח", ותזכה להפיץ מעיינותיך חוצה. וידוע דברי המלך שלמה במשלי "אוהב מוסר אוהב דעת ושונא תוכחות בער". ומפאת קוצר הזמן לא הספקתי לעבור על כל הכתוב "וחזקה על חבר שיוציא דבר מתוקן".

בברכת
התורה:

ידידך שאול מסלתון
הכהן

ירושלים: _____

בס"ד

To Our dear beloved אשה and בעל who loves 'ה
R' Eliyahu נ"י

I am very happy to see your hard work and efforts in putting out
beautiful ספרי קודש and מחזק ונותן to guide a person's daily life
with חיזוק and אמונה. As we know Chacham Ovadia Yosef זצ"ל
encouraged very much writing and publishing ספרי קודש, and he gave
many הסכמות – endorsements to ספרים encouraging the beauty of
writing and publishing ספרי קודש. Especially in our world that there
is so much material on non proper ideas it is very important to
write and encourage the spreading of ספרי קודש all over. The
בן איש חי has an entire beautiful section on the importance of
writing and publishing ספרי קודש, and he brings that writing
and publishing ספרי קודש is like bringing a קרבן to ה'. The
רמב"ן tells us that putting out ספרים is one of those מצות that
a person reaps the reward even when he is not active, but
others are getting a הנאה from it. It is beautiful that you
have put time in being מחזק הדור and as we know that
כל המזכה את הרבים אין חטא בא על ידו. May ה' give you
the כוח to being מחזק הרבים for many years.

May ה' bless you and your entire great family with
all the ברכות and מתנות from your children to be going in
the beautiful way of תורה הקדושה from health, happiness and
נחת אמיתי. אמן וכן יהי רצון.

Beloved Rabbe – Sinai Yakoban

רח' הקבלן 34, ירושלים 93874, ישראל, Rechov Hakablan 34 Jerusalem 93874, Israel.
e-mail: levaharon101@gmail.com lev_aharon@012.net.il N.Y. Line: (718) 663-0446, Fax: 02-653-7811 :פקס, Tel: 02-651-4431 :טל

THE VISION OF LIFE 2

YESHIVAT LEV AHARON
IN MEMORY OF AHARON LANIADO A"H
ע.ר. 580454619
EIN: 13-3706282

Rabbi David Laniado
Rosh Hayeshiva

Aslan Safdeye
President

Administration
Jack Dayon
Allison Safdieh
Bina Chrem

Alumni Chairman
Raymond Kishk

כ"א אייר תשע"ט

To my dear student R' Eliyahu Kbabieh, הי"ו

It is always a great simcha to see young people publishing and spreading their divrei Torah. How much more so and exiting it is when you remember how just a few years ago a talmid just starting off his learning career, has now gotten to the level of printing his own chiddushim. This is for sure in the merit of his toiling in Torah and his pure heart to understand the right way to go in avodat Hashem. Knowing the author, I am sure that his intentions are לשם שמים, to help others in the right path through things that he experiences on his own. I also know him as a tremendous בעל חסד and the biggest chesed that you can do for another is to give them spiritual support. This sefer has a special segulah of דברים היוצאים מן הלב נכנסים ללב. At last, I would like to end off with a simple beracha that the writer be zocheh that many people read his sefer and come closer to Hashem through his words.

Rabbi David Laniado
Rosh Yeshiva

Israel Campus: 34 Hakablan, PO Box 43215, Jerusalem Israel 91430
Tel // +972-2-651-4431 // Fax +972-2-653-7811
US line: (in Israel) 718-689-1667 // office@levaharon.com
US Office: PO Box 275, West Long Branch, NJ 07764 // 917-588-6415 // nyoffice@levaharon.com

In Memory of Jack Adjmi ע״ה

Rabbi David Ozeri
Rabbi David Sutton

בס״ד

I would like to give a ברכה to Eliyahu Kbabieh to continue on his path of working hard in being מחזק others. Eliyahu is constantly growing and striving to achieve greater heights in his עבודת ה'.
May 'ה bless him with continued סייעתא דשמיא and give in success in all that he does.

ברכה והצלחה

David Ashear

Contents

Letter from the Author xxiii
Introduction xxv

1. The True Light 1
2. The Truth of Mankind 2
3. Yom Kippur Is Like Purim 3
4. The Value of a Misva 5
5. Danger of Lashon Hara #1 7
6. Don't Look at Others 9
7. Thoughts 11
8. Talk to Hashem 13
9. Every Jew Has a Spark 15
10. Accept Your Suffering with Love 18
11. Peace in the World 19
12. Watch Your Mouth 20
13. Be Happy in Your Heart 21
14. Tsisit 22
15. Who's Really Happy? 23
16. Hashem's Kindness 24
17. Guard Your Eyes 25
18. Life Is Full of Tests 26
19. Keep Your Words to Yourself 28
20. Hashem Loves You 29
21. Mesillat Yesharim Chapter 1 31

22.	Mesillat Yesharim Chapter 2	32
23.	The Light of a Person	33
24.	Trust in Hashem	34
25.	Torah Was Given Only to the Jews	36
26.	From the Heart	37
27.	Turn from Bad	38
28.	Who Will Help?	39
29.	Learn the Torah with Compassion	40
30.	Hashem Wants to Hear from You	42
31.	Watch Your Ways	43
32.	The Power of Being Humble	45
33.	Prayers Is Your Medication	46
34.	Open Your Heart	48
35.	If I Am Not for Myself, Who Will Be for Me?	49
36.	The Second Yehi Ratzon in Berchot Hashachar	51
37.	A Good Heart	52
38.	It's a Gift	54
39.	Hashem Hears You	56
40.	Hashem's Plan	57
41.	Praise Hashem	59
42.	Only Hashem Himself	60
43.	Give It Up	61
44.	The Power of Saying Birkat Hamazon	63
45.	The Power of Speech	64
46.	Torah Is Life	66
47.	Stay Away from a Bad Friend	68
48.	Start Now	69
49.	Stay Away from Bad	70
50.	The Spark Is in You	72
51.	Torah Erases Your Sins	73

52. You Won't Come to Sin	74
53. The Power of Strength	75
54. Ask for Knowledge	76
55. Come Back	77
56. Don't Panic	78
57. Hashem's Power	79
58. Danger of Lashon Hara #2	81
59. Being Patient	82
60. Pray in Shul	83
61. What's the Real Medicine?	85
62. Fear Hashem	86
63. Learn from the Tiniest Thing	87
64. Love Hashem	88
65. Pure Mindset	89
66. Toiling Is What Counts	90
67. Hashem's Mercy	91
68. Look at Yourself	92
69. Where Are You Headed?	93
70. It's About Love	94
71. The Real Vision	95
72. Regret the Bad, Not the Good	96
73. The Power of Embarrassment	97
74. A Smile Can Change Your Day	99
75. Clean Mindset	100
76. How to Gain Purity	101
77. Hashem Is with a Tsaddik	102
78. Engage in Torah	103
79. Do It for Hashem	104
80. Pirkei Avot	105
81. The True Desire	106

82.	A Tsaddik Is Like a Tree 107
83.	Who's Really Going to Heal Me? 108
84.	Bitachon Is the Source of Everything 109
85.	We All Have One Father 111
86.	Allow Hashem to Fight Your Problems 113
87.	What Are We Living For? 115
88.	Return to the Torah 116
89.	The Light of a Person 118
90.	There's No One Like Hashem Who Is Like Hashem? 120
91.	The Fruit of Life 122
92.	Stay Happy 123
93.	Don't Take Revenge 125
94.	Don't Be Frustrated 126
95.	People Need Chizuk 128
96.	The Danger of Technology 129
97.	Cry Out 130
98.	The Importance of Having a Realization 131
99.	Cling to Hashem 132
100.	Perform Misvot in This World 133

Biography 135

Letter from the Author

I thank Hashem for giving me the ability to write the second *sefer* of *The Vision of Life*. If it were not for Hashem helping me and giving me the ideas of what to write, I would not have been able to publish another book.

When I was writing these messages, I didn't have the intention to publish it. But then I realized that this book is meant to help people and myself become closer to Hashem and to continue striving for the truth of life.

The Vision of Life Volume 2 is a continuation of the first book that came out mid-March 2016, *The Vision of Life*.

Introduction

Pirkei Avot 2:8 states: The more you feed the soul with Torah, the more life you have.

To have life, you first must have Torah in you. Torah is what brings a person to life.

***

The Gemara (*Kiddushin* 30b) states: When a person is engaged in Torah, he won't be trapped by the evil inclination.

***

Tehillim 27:7 states: Hear my voice and answer my prayers. When it says, "Hear my prayers and answer me," it is showing Klal Yisrael that if they call out to Hashem, He will answer their voice. Ever since I came out with the first volume, I would pray to Hashem for the ability to continue writing *mussar* and to be able to change my ways for the better.

***

Tehillim 1:1 states: Praiseworthy is the person who does not go in the evil direction.

This book is meant to help everyone stay away from the evil path and realize the good that Hashem does for each and every one of us.

***

The Vision of Life, Volume 2 will help you grow in Hashem's ways and keep you away from the bad in life.

1. The True Light

The question is, what is the true light of a person? Every *Jew* has a pure *neshamah*. It's in your hands if you want to see the true light.

People think that buying the best car is the true light of life.

In *Tehillim* it says, "They have eyes." Having eyes that Hashem gave you, you should see the true light, and that true light is the Holy Torah & to go in Hashem's way.

When a person is engaged in Torah, he will see the truth in his personal life.

However, if Heaven forbid a person doesn't have Torah, he won't see the true light of life. When a person learns Torah, he is feeding the *neshamah* and that is the only thing the *neshamah* needs is Torah.

When a person is not learning Torah, he starves his *neshamah*, because the only thing it wants is Torah & misvot!!

When you're starving, what is the first thing you do? The first thing is on your mind is, "I am starving—I need to eat."

That is how we should examine our *neshamot*. We should always feed them with Torah and misvot.

The true light of every single *Yid* who is out there—whether Sephardic, Syrian, Ashkenazi, Israeli, Moroccan, or all of the above—at the end we are all one nation. You need Torah in your life and if you don't have Torah in your life, start now, because it's never too late.

Hashem is waiting for you to bring the true light into your personal life and that is learning Torah and performing misvot in this world.

Torah and misvot bring true light.

2. The Truth of Mankind

Every person wants to be a true person but you can't just say that; you must know *how* to become a true person. The way a person becomes a true person is by speaking the truth and toiling in Torah and misvot.

A person develops by telling the truth and learning the Torah; that is how you make yourself true.

The *sheker* of a person is when he runs to the *gashmiyut* and thinks, "This is the truth of life." If a person will have a clear vision in his life, he will realize that the only thing he'll be taking from this world is the Torah and misvot that are only performed in this world.

The *gashmiyut* that is out in the world is all going to stay in Olam Ha'ze.

Mesillat Yesharim writes that the reason why there is *gashmiyut* in this world is to make a person go further from Hashem.

Every morning we say in our tefillah that if we keep the misvot in this world; we'll merit to live with good blessing in this world and in the World to Come.

Every deed that a person performs in this world earns him *Olam Haba*; every deed that you perform in this world counts, whether it is bad or good.

This is the biggest investment that you can make: Hashem gave the us the Torah and 613 misvot to perform.

Focus on one misva that you can do right; the more you do that, more misvot will come to you: *Misva ha"ba misva*.

To become a true person, speak the truth.

3. Yom Kippur Is Like Purim

The month of Adar is the happiest month of the year.

We are supposed to be extra happy in this month of the year.

Adar is a special month, and our sages tell us that any court case you have pending should be scheduled in this month of the year.

Every person should hold strong in this month of Adar, since this is also the time of the year when the *yetzer hara* gets stronger, not allowing a person to feel extra happy. In addition, the *yetzer hara* always wants to make a person feel down or look at the past instead of the future; that is all in fact the *yetzer hara*.

It states in Tehillim, "The wicked person runs after a righteous person to kill." The word "wicked" refers to the evil inclination that always chases the good people to try to wipe us out, but the most important thing is that we stay strong and fight that evil inclination.

There's a famous gemara in *Sukkah daf* 52: Rabbi Yitzhak says, A person's *yetzer hara* gets stronger every day and wants you to only do bad.

We all should have an open vision and not fall in the pit of the *yetzer hara*. Every day it gets stronger, but at the same time we have the ability to knock it out. We fight the *yetzer hara* by keeping ourselves busy with the Torah and performing *chesed* in this world. We can't stop; if we are performing good deeds, we must continue till the end, because as soon as we stop, the *yetzer hara* is going to affect us.

Our sages tell us that the prayer of Minha on the day of Purim is so powerful that anything we ask of Hashem with full sincerity, He will grant.

Purim is a day when everyone has an obligation to be happy more than ever before.

On Yom Kippur, we all fast, not eating for 24 hours straight; no one dares to eat or drink unless it's a matter of life and death for which you must break the fast. On Purim, we should feel the same way: no one should enter Purim in a mood that is upset at something.

We are so lucky to have this special month called Adar and to have Purim.

We should always be happy in our lives.

4. The Value of a Misva

We are so lucky that Hashem made us into a Jewish nation.

Hashem gave us 613 misvot and the value of one misva can connect us to Hashem.

Performing just one misva is worth more than any *gashmiyut* out there in the world, and the reason for that is because for one misva you are rewarded for eternity in *Olam Haba*. One physical thing that you have in this world cannot compare to just one misva—that is the power of one single misva.

Each misva that we perform in this world corresponds to one limb in our body: We have 613 limbs that represent 248 negative actions and 365 positive actions.

When a misva comes your way, always grab it and perform it completely. Don't push it away and say, I will perform it later on, because you don't know for sure that this misva will come back. That is why if any misva that comes your way, grab it and do it quickly.

Pirkei Avot states, "Consider the cost of a misva against the reward." Performing misvot should be for the sake of Hashem, not for the intention of getting a reward. You don't need a reward in this world; know that you are gaining yourself *Olam Haba* each time you perform a misva. The most important thing is don't stop, keep going till the end.

One sin, Heaven forbid, that anyone does is a loss to the person. He doesn't receive anything good but the bad, Heaven forbid. Of course, no one wants that to happen, so in order to have good in your life, keep on performing good deeds.

I will conclude with a story I heard from Rabbi Duvi Benshusan.

A student once asked the Chofetz Chaim a question. He asked, "What will be good in Hashem's eyes?"

The Chofetz Chaim responded, "Performing *chesed*, because when you perform *chesed* for others, Hashem will show *chesed* to you."

The value of a misva will help a person reach greatness.

5. Danger of Lashon Hara #1

A person should be cautious with the way he speaks to people. Why?

Because if a person is speaking to someone and then, all of a sudden, he spoke bad about another person, that is considered *lashon hara*, evil speech, which is one of the worst things in the Torah.

Many people talk to their friends and they say words that can really hurt a person; even if it is meant as a joke, it's still not allowed to do.

People have feelings, and even if they say, "It's okay, it doesn't bother me," still you should train yourself to speak properly. You should learn the laws of *lashon hara* because it can really destroy a person's life.

A famous gemara in *Bava Kama* states that a person should rather throw himself or herself into a burning fire rather than embarrass someone in public. The reason is a person has a heart and whatever you say, that person will always remember what you said.

The next time you're about to say *lashon hara*, train yourself not to do so, because you don't want, Heaven forbid, to cause any problems.

Our speech is so powerful that a person should guide his or her mouth every day on the way we speak to people, whether to a Jew or a non-Jew. Make your mouth pure and speak only good.

If you are invited to dinner with family or friends and you realize that the food is too salty, instead of rudely commenting, "Wow, this food is way too salty," instead be thankful to the people who invited you and give a positive response: "The food is so delicious! Thanks for having me."

One main reason the Second Temple was destroyed is because of baseless hatred and speaking *lashon hara*. Therefore, if we would analyze our words and think before we speak, with Hashem's help we can see the building of the Third Temple.

The Chofetz Chaim says, "Cursed is a person who attacks a person in secret."

This teaches us a lesson in life: Many people go to a wedding or a bar misva or any event; later, instead of Heaven forbid speaking bad after you leave, speak only good. Even if you didn't enjoy the event, keep it to yourself, and next time you'll know how to handle the situation better.

Don't be a secret person who behind closed doors speaks bad about another person, because the Chofetz Chaim's words teach us that a person is cursed if he does so.

Tehillim it states, "Who is a person who desires life and who is a person who loves his or her days?"

Tehillim answers, "A person who watches the way he speaks to people and the one who guards his mouth from evil speech."

A person who doesn't speak any bad about anybody out there will always be happy and relaxed with everything that is going on. But when a person speaks *lashon hara*, he is first destroying the person he is talking about and second, he is frustrating himself by talking and talking.

A person who wants to be happy all his life and see good in life, doesn't speak bad but rather speaks only good.

6. Don't Look at Others

A person shouldn't look at others and say, "If that person isn't praying, I am not going to pray," and "If that person is on his phone, I am going to use my phone." That is the biggest mistake people make; don't look at others and start doing bad.

The first thing everyone needs to know is that each person should be responsible with everything he does. Of course, it's in our hands to do good in this world, so stop relying on other people and do things on your own.

Don't look at others and say, "Oh, they didn't go to shul, I don't have to go." That is a big mistake and a really bad character trait. Each person must do his or her own task to complete his or her purpose in the world, which means that everyone has a specific job to do. For example, if a person is working for a company and the boss tells the employee that his hours are from 9 a.m. to 7 p.m., that employee has to be responsible to be on time. He shouldn't look at others and say that since another employee comes late every day, why shouldn't he? No, each one must do what he has to do. Just as in life, each one must do his best and the rest is in Hashem's hands.

Boys who reach the age of 13 have the status of being responsible for all their actions, which includes:

Going to shul, putting on *tefillin* every morning, and not missing a day of davening and wearing *tefillin*

Being really cautious to make sure not to do any sin, Heaven forbid.

Girls who reach the age of 12 also have the status of being responsible for all their actions, which includes:

Making sure they perform *chesed* in this world to earn the Next World

Making sure to pray to Hashem once or twice a day.

Everyone, including myself, should not look at others and start talking and saying why is he or her doing that and so on so forth, because looking at others in a negative way will also bring the character trait of jealousy. However, looking at others in a positive way and giving them a nice comment with a smile is great. Again, looking at others and saying, "Look, their talking in shul, why can't I?" is something that each person should not do. Do not follow the bad example of others.

There's one thing for which you can look at others and gain the right type of jealousy and inspiration—that is looking at a person learning the Torah and performing good deeds. They are doing something good in this world.

When you see someone who is learning or doing good in this world, try to be inspired by that person.

7. Thoughts

A person sometimes has thoughts of committing a sin; sometimes we're blinded by the evil inclination and many people don't realize that Hashem knows all thoughts of human beings. As it states in *Tehillim*, Hashem knows how people are thinking; anytime a person is facing these thoughts of committing a sin, it's a challenge that he is going through. The way to avoid these thoughts is to keep your mind pure by not looking at disgusting things.

Every day, we say (twice as a *d'Orayta* and four times as a *d'Rabanan*) the prayer of *Shema Yisrael*. We say the words, "Don't stray after what your heart or eyes desire." Once a person looks at things he shouldn't be looking at, he's going to start to have bad thoughts that will cause him to sin.

We should all realize that Hashem is watching us every step we take in our lives. Instead of having negative thoughts and thinking evil, have the good thoughts that Hashem gave you a life, a house, parents who are there to protect you and do what's best for you. Realize that the biggest gift of all is just that Hashem gave us life. Instead of being down and not wanting to do good, look at the positive side, because that negative feeling is the evil inclination that wants to harm you.

Every time we overcome these negative thoughts, Hashem is going to reward us in the Next World Train your mind to always think positive.

Why does Hashem make us have these tests? Hashem gives people test because He knows that we can overcome them. Hashem doesn't give anybody a test in this world that he can't overcome.

When a person is undergoing a test, he should always know that he really can overcome it by being a fighter and sticking with pure thoughts and actions.

We should all have positive thoughts, only thinking to do good in this world and making Hashem proud.

8. Talk to Hashem

The best thing a person can do is talk to Hashem directly. The same way you're sitting and talking with your friends, you can sit down and talk to Hashem; Hashem wants to hear from you.

Pour your heart out and talk to Hashem with all your problems.

Imagine you want to meet someone because you want to talk to them to help you out with your problems; often they'll tell you that you have to wait until it's your turn. However, whenever you have a problem you can talk directly to Hashem; He wants to help—you just have to believe it.

If a person truthfully wants to get close to Hashem, all he or she has to do is call upon him in truth, as it states: Hashem is close to all who call upon Him in truth.

A person who calls upon on Hashem in truth, Hashem will become close to him.

Anytime something is bothering you, close your eyes and speak to Hashem. Don't carry your problems yourself; throw your problems to Hashem. Don't stress about it or drive yourself crazy; rather, speak to Hashem sincerely. He wants to help you, but you have to ask and talk to Hashem.

Many people, when praying to Hashem, start thinking negative thoughts that they are not worthy of praying because they just committed a sin. No, it doesn't matter what you did; Hashem is judging you at the time what you're doing now—praying sincerely for His help.

Praying is the biggest investment out there—and it's free of charge. No need to pay or travel; all you have to do is talk to Hashem.

The more you talk to Hashem, the more you're connecting yourself to the King Who owns everything.

If we would live our lives like this, talking to Hashem every day, we'll see Hashem is in our lives every day.

Start talking to Hashem and pour out your heart.

Hashem should give all of us the feeling of closeness to Hashem, wanting to talk to Him and realizing everything is Hashem giving to us using earthly messengers.

Talk to Hashem today.

9. Every Jew Has a Spark

If a person committed a sin, Heaven forbid, he shouldn't give up and say to himself, "I sinned so much, I am no longer worthy to learn or pray." When a person thinks that way and say those words, it's the *yetzer hara* trying to influence him. Even if you fell so many times, get back up and continue fighting until you get it right. By doing that, you're lighting the spark in you.

Mesillat Yesharim says that a person has to have an idea to be cautious not to do bad things. A person has an obligation to watch himself physically and spirituality, and the reason for that is that every single Jew has that spark in him or her. In order to light that spark, you have to perform good deeds and learn the Torah.

The more a person places himself or herself in sinful situations and goes to places they shouldn't go, they are placing that spark into darkness. They are making it so dark that there's no spark. You want that spark to light—it's called a spark, which means *to light*— to light the world with the Torah and misvot.

A famous parable explains this point:

A person is not feeling well and he goes to the doctor. The doctor tells the patient, "I will write you a prescription; take it once a day."

The person takes that prescription and throws it away and doesn't listen to the doctor

What is this person doing to himself or herself?

Hashem gave us the Torah to grow with it learn from it and change our old ways. By doing that, you're making yourself spark on the inside.

I heard this story a few years ago from Rabbi Meyer Chemtob:

There was a boy named Binyamin; his life was full of Torah and performing misvot. He came from a religious home and went to yeshiva. After he had been doing so well, his *yetzer hara* awakened strongly in him and Binyamin fell into a big pit. He went to the Rabbi of the yeshiva and said, "Rabbi, there's no point in me being religious anymore. I don't want to wear *tsisit* or kippa. I'm done; I want to live my life how I want it to be." The rabbi looks at the boy, thinking, "What happened to you?"

Binyamin starts to yell, "Enough! I'm done!" He takes his kippa and throws it away.

The parents realized that their child is in bad trouble and they try to help, but they have no success.

Binyamin comes homes one day with tattoos on his hand and all over his body. The father looks at the child, trying to help him and Binyamin disrespects his father. The father got so upset that he told Binyamin, "I'm sorry, but there's no place for you in this house."

Binyamin, with his bad attitude, smirks at his father and says, "No problem!"

Binyamin go upstairs, packs his stuff, and moves to Los Angeles.

He goes to many clubs and at one club he drank so much that he mistakenly he hit a gangster. They beat him up till he was gushing blood.

Binyamin left the club crying, shaking, and not knowing what to do. He had no choice but to call his father. Binyamin was trembling as he picked up the phone and started to dial the numbers. When his father picks up the phone, the son said, "Abba, I am so sorry for all the trouble I got into. I just got beat up and I feel so depressed. Abba, I am sorry, I want to come back home."

The father tells Binyamin, "Get on the next flight and I will see you in a few hours."

Binyamin is on the plane, nervously praying to Hashem to help him approach his parents the right way. He was praying nonstop and crying.

At the airport, Binyamin saw his parents, and the only words that came out of his mouth were *Shema Yisrael Hashem Elokeinu Hashem Ehad.*

Whatever you did in the past, no matter what sin you did, you can always come back to Hashem and become who you really are—because at the end of the day each person has that spark of Hashem.

10. Accept Your Suffering with Love

When a person is suffering, he should know that Hashem is making that decree and he should accept it with love. Whether it's missing a city bus or the train or a car ride and you feel the frustration, consider that is a small affliction and it is atonement for your past sins.

Every suffering a person accepts with love gains the person *Olam Haba* for it. Every pain you are going through should be considered the biggest gift, because those sufferings are gaining you *Olam Haba* and those suffering are atonements for your sins.

One reason we face suffering is that Hashem wants to see how we are going to react to these afflictions: are we going to start complaining or we going to accept them with love?

Each suffering that a person goes through and handles it the right way is the person reaching to greatness.

Suffering brings a person to perfection.

11. Peace in the World

When a person has peace with others, everything will go smoothly, but if, Heaven forbid, a person doesn't have peace, that person is losing on so many things.

Each person should run after peace by making peace with his fellow. By doing that, you're fulfilling the words in the mishna.

Each person should be like the students of Aharon, who loved peace and changed fighting for peace. Our Sages teach us that anytime Aharon saw someone fighting or arguing, he would make peace between them.

Bringing peace to the world is something we all must do. Bringing *shalom*, peace, between our friends that is the only way we can bring them close to Torah; without peace it will be much harder to bring people close to the Torah.

The most important thing is to have peace in the world; something important about performing *shalom* in the world is that you're bringing Hashem into the picture because *Shalom* is one of Hashem's Names!

Start bring peace to the world, bring peace to families and friends, and with that in mind we will see Mashiach.

12. Watch Your Mouth

A person should really be cautious about the way he speaks to people. Words are so powerful that we must be careful with the way we speak to people.

In Tehillim it states, "Who is the men that loves his life and loves his days?"

David HaMelech answers, "Watch your mouth from evil." What is the purpose of all this?

A person who wants to live a life full of enjoyment should not speak bad about anyone, because when a person comes to the point of speaking harsh about this person and that person, he is placing himself in danger—all the blessings he is supposed to receive will all turn into a curse.

The Chofetz Chaim *zt'l* said the reason the Temple was destroyed was because of people hating each other and speaking *lashon hara*. So too, if we all keep our mouths clean and not speak bad but rather speak good about people, then we can see the rebuilding of the Temple.

Turn away from speaking bad and start speaking good.

13. Be Happy in Your Heart

A person's heart should always be happy

When a person is performing something for his fellow person, let it be from the heart, meaning that you're happy to do the act.

When your parents or Rabbis tell you to perform something, let it come directly from the heart that you truthfully want to do it, because when it's coming from the heart, you'll feel amazed and you will want to continue performing good deeds.

When you pray to Hashem and learn Torah, let it come from the heart, because Hashem wants it to be from the heart. How do you feel when you're serving Hashem? Are you doing it from the heart or are you doing it because everyone else is?

Berachot Yerushalmi states, "Those who give their heart and eyes are truly to Hashem."

A person should give everything to Hashem. When praying and performing good deeds, let them come from the heart.

14. Tsisit

Some people wear *tsisit* and some don't.

The truth is, every male Jew is supposed to wear *tsisit* (halacha in *Shulchan Aruch*).

The biggest protection out there is a four-cornered garment with *tsisit*. Each time you wear it, you earn reward for every second it is on you.

A person makes excuses for why he doesn't want to wear *tsisit*. He says it's too itchy and the weather is too hot; in truth, that is the *yetzer hara* of a person talking

This is the easiest misva in this world. It costs only pennies and you can earn *Olam Haba* by wearing *tsisit*. A person should truly accept on himself to wear *tsisit*.

When a person wears the *tsisit* and stares at the *tsisit*, it will save him from sinning.

The Ben Ish Chai *zt'l* writes that the *gematria* of *tsisit* is 613, the same as the number of misvot that Hashem gave us.

Wearing a garment of *tsisit* can make a person realize that there are 613 misvot out there—and you can earn one by wearing one.

Don't forget your bulletproof vest.

15. Who's Really Happy?

A person thinks that having the best car out there is going to bring true happiness. This is not called true happiness; it's called *sheker*, falsehood. This type of happiness is false happiness.

To gain real happiness is not so easy; it's hard. You have to work on it to be happy. To gain happiness, you must sit down and learn the Torah and hear mussar. By doing that, you'll earn the truth of being alive and you'll also gain true happiness.

A short parable:

A child buys a game and the child is excited. The child plays with the game for a few weeks until he says, "Uchh, this game is getting boring. I want to buy a new game." It goes on and on; that is the *yetzer hara* that always makes a person excited about things in this world, and it's all a waste of time that just wants us to take us further from Hashem.

The only thing will bring a person true happiness is Torah; the Torah is the only thing that will be with a person for the rest of his or her life.

Each person should pray to Hashem to have true happiness and to learn the Torah with full passion.

Pirkei Avot 2:7 states, "The more a person learns the Torah, the more he has life."

Torah brings a person to true life in this world.

16. Hashem's Kindness

The *Chovot HaLevavot, Shaar Habechina* says that a person is complete by having everything he need. It says: All the things that benefit a person is that he is provided with hands and fingers. The fingers benefit you because you can write words of Torah with them.

You can write is the biggest gift itself.

Hashem gave us gifts: Hands. Legs. A mouth. That itself is the biggest gift and we must use them wisely. Using them the right way is by performing good in the world.

Hashem gave each person his or her own thing; you can do the things in this world of your own free will. By performing good in the world, you are blessing yourself and blessing the world. When a person takes the kindness of Hashem and performs good in this world, he will earn *Olam Haba* at the end.

Many people say, "Hashem is harming me; I can't find my shidduch" or "I can't find a job," and the list goes on. The fact that you're living is the biggest gift from Hashem, and Hashem has timing and places for everyone.

Hashem did not forget about you! Don't forget about the great kindness Hashem does for you on a daily basis.

Instead of looking at the negative side, look at the positive side of all that Hashem has been doing for you.

17. Guard Your Eyes

How powerful it is to watch our pure eyes that Hashem has given us.

Hashem gave us eyes to see the good, not the bad!

When you're in the streets walking to get to your place, be careful with those pure eyes that Hashem gave you.

It states in the *Shema Yisrael* in the paragraph beginning *Vayomer*, "And he said," "Don't stray after your heart and your eyes."

Every single Jew should have this in his or her mind when walking in the streets: remember not to look at improper things. Because if, Heaven forbid, you do look, your heart is going to desire it and you will come to sin.

Guarding one's eyes will see blessing and it's an *et ratzon*, time when it is good to pray: Every time you control your eyes, you can ask Hashem for anything.

When you control your eyes, they are having the biggest celebration for you in Heaven!

Control your eyes today and you will see a big difference in your life. You'll see clarity in life; you will know how to make proper decisions in life—just control your eyes.

To see Hashem in your life, you must guard your eyes.

18. Life Is Full of Tests

Everyone wants to become great and be successful in life in the fastest way, but sometimes when a person is trying to do things quickly to become great, he falls "down the hill" spiritually.

A person is supposed to view life by taking things step by step.

In *Parashat Vayeishev*, Yaakov placed stones around his head and went to sleep. He dreamed he saw a ladder with angels going up and down on it.

What's the lesson?

Don't angels have wings? Why were the angels going up and down on a ladder?

The lesson we should learn from it is to live our lives by taking it step by step, one at a time.

The Jewish people told Hashem, "Ribono Shel Olam, You know how strong the *yetzer hara* is. How can we conquer it?"

Hashem said, "Send the *yetzer hara* away step by step in this world and I will totally remove the *yetzer hara* in the future."

Today, improve in one thing; tomorrow, improve a drop more, until you become a great person.

The midrash writes that when one sets up a mission to become a greater person, he is not always going to make a final and decision to change.

Each day a person is supposed to increase his or her steps every single day.

The midrash writes that you should only focus on the small amount of improvement, because these small good deeds that you're performing will add up and you will be successful.

I will conclude with a parable that we can learn from:

A person is addicted to cigarettes. Every day he smokes two packs. One day, his wife tells him, "Listen, this is not healthy for you. You must stop smoking. The way to stop is not to say, 'I'm going to stop smoking right now,' but rather to cut down every day. Every day you cut down a cigarette until you completely stop smoking."

The moral applies to all of us: Whatever you're having trouble with and you want to stop, you should cut down slowly, little by little, till you get it right.

Life is full of tests, but you have the ability to overcome them.

19. Keep Your Words to Yourself

We go through life meeting people, socializing with people, doing business with people, all of which is a great achievement.

When you have a conversation with people, always be positive with the way they are. If you see something and you think he or she looks bad—keep it to yourself!

There's no need to pour out the bad thought and embarrass the person, Heaven forbid.

We should learn the concept of keeping our words to ourselves.

That means controlling ourselves not to speak any bad or negative comments, Heaven forbid.

Keep your words to yourself.

20. Hashem Loves You

Hashem is the only One Who chose us and nobody else.

Hashem is the master of the universe Who loves you more than you love yourself.

When a person, Heaven forbid, commits a sin, the first thing on his mind is, "I'm done, I can't learn Torah anymore, I'm too embarrassed. I can't, Hashem dislikes me."

Heaven forbid!

Hashem is the master of the universe Who has more mercy than anybody else, so even if you fall, get back on your feet and repent.

In my first book, *The Vision of Life*, I mentioned in the name of Rabbi Ezra Dayan that the game is really to fight!

Rabbi Ezra Dayan added something more: When a person is fighting against his *yetzer hara*, he's a winner!

When you are a fighter, you're a winner!

When you're having a bad day, know in yourself that it's the biggest kindness that Hashem is doing for you.

Whatever Hashem does for you is 100 percent for your best, because He loves you!

A parable is brought down in the *Chovot HaLevavot, Shaar Bitachon*:

A father takes his child to the doctor to get a flu shot. The doctor comes into the room and all of a sudden, the father holds the child down.

The child looks up at his father and thinks, "Why is my daddy holding me tight?"

Then the doctor gives the child his flu shot and the child thinks, "You're my father and you're letting this person hurt me!" The child starts crying! In truth, this shot is for the best for the child.

It's the same with Hashem: Sometimes we go through a struggle in life, but in truth Hashem is doing it for our best.

21. Mesillat Yesharim Chapter 1

The first chapter of *Mesillat Yesharim* tells us that a person's purpose in this world is to do the *avodat Hashem*, the service of Hashem.

"*She'adam lo nivera ella l'hitanag al Hashem*"

A person wasn't created for no reason; rather, a person was created to enjoy what Hashem gave him. Hashem gave us the Torah and misvot to perform them in this world; as we perform good deeds in this world, we earn for ourselves *Olam Haba*, the World to Come

A person can perform good deeds ONLY in this world. That is why if you were placed in this world, toil in misvot as much as you can—because you are building your *Olam Haba*.

Gemara *Eruvin* states, "*Hayom lastom yumachar mekebel sachar*—Perform the misvot today and tomorrow you will be rewarded."

When you are engaged in misvot, you are earning your ticket to *Olam Haba*.

To enter *Olam Haba*, you need *Olam Ha'ze*, this world. *Olam Ha'ze* is for your own benefit to do *avodat Hashem*.

The purpose of life is to toil in misvot and learning Torah.

22. Mesillat Yesharim Chapter 2

The second chapter of *Mesillat Yesharim* teaches a major lesson in life: each person must open his eyes and see if his actions are good or bad. That is being cautious, and we all have the obligation to be careful with our actions.

The chapter brings an idea on how we are supposed to examine our actions. Just as we wouldn't go near a wild animal, so too we should distance ourselves from sins and danger.

This chapter gives us the realization that each person is placed in this world to toil in misvot and to learn Torah. When we do that, we are earning *Olam Haba*.

The Hebrew word *zehirut* teaches us something; if we look at the word, we will see that each letter means something:

Be careful Hashem
Is watching
You
Do
Teshuva

That is the meaning of the letters of the word *zehirut*.

Start looking at your actions whether they are good or bad; if they are bad, refrain from them and start doing good.

23. The Light of a Person

Keep the light burning constantly.

The Dubno Magid says that the *ner tamid*, continual light, that the Kohen Gadol would light in the Menorah in the *Beit HaMikdash* was the symbol of Torah.

Mishlei 6:23 states, "For a commandment is a lamp and the Torah is light." This teaches us a lesson in life: a misva we perform in this world is a candle, and the Torah is the Light.

We should all realize that all the time we spend learning the Torah and performing misvot, we are making the candles light up—and we should never allow the *yetzer hara* to interfere in our lives.

Everyone who is here in this world and goes to a class is doing a misva.

When you learn the Torah, the candle that you make by coming to class is lit with your learning.

24. Trust in Hashem

On a recent Erev Shabbat, I directly saw Hashem's hand helping me and knew that He was listening to my prayers. This is the timeline of what happened that day:

12:00 p.m. Friday afternoon, while driving to the suit store to buy a nice suit in honor of Shabbat, I was talking to Hashem, asking Him to help me find the perfect suit.

12:10 p.m. While I was waiting at the street light on Avenue S and McDonald I spoke to Hashem, saying, "Hashem, even though it's 12:10 and I still have a few hours till Shabbat, help me get there on time so I shouldn't rush through bringing in the Shabbat."

I opened my eyes and I saw that from Avenue S and McDonald, all the way to my destination, all the street lights we're green. (*Yad Hashem* the first time.)

Before making a left turn, while I stopped at the light, I closed my eyes again and said, "Hashem, just like You made all the lights green for me, please help me find a good parking spot near the store."

I opened up my eyes and made the left turn. I looked around and found a perfect parking spot—I didn't even have to pay the meter! I parked the car and got out of the car, saying, "Hashem, thank You so much! I love you, Hashem!" (*Yad Hashem* the second time.)

I was about to enter the suit store when I got a call from my mom. She said, "Hi, Eli! Where are you?"

I responded, "I am at a suit store and I am buying a suit in honor of Shabbat."

She asked, "Why did you think about this now? You should've gone last night."

I said, "Mom, I'm here, and with Hashem's help I'm going to look for a nice suit."

She asked, "How much money do you have?" I told her that I had 130 dollars and she responded, "Eli, you're very funny if you think you're going to find a suit for that price! It's impossible!" I said, "Mom, Hashem will help me."

I ended the call and I closed my eyes. I said, "Hashem, please help me find a suit for the money I have."

In the store, I asked one of the men working there, "Hi, sir, would you be able to help me find a suit?" He said it would be his pleasure to help me.

I closed my eyes and said, "Hashem, he's a messenger, and I am relying on You, Hashem."

The man showed me all the suits and I chose one to try on. It fit perfectly, tailor made from Hashem. I said to myself, "This suit is worth 180 dollars for sure!"

Still, I didn't give up hope and said, "Hashem, please help me out.

I'm still relying on You." I looked at the price and the suit was only 100 dollars. (*Yad Hashem* the third time.)

Finally, before I was about to leave the store, I wanted to buy a nice tie in honor of Shabbat. I said, "Hashem, please help me find a nice tie to match the suit."

Baruch Hashem, I found the perfect tie, and I was waiting on line to pay and thanking Hashem for the great gifts He did for me (*Yad Hashem* the fourth time.)

The subtotal for my suit and tie was 107 dollars, which has the gematria (numerical value) of HASHEM'S NAME four times (104) and the word BO (3), totaling 107 dollars.

Four times Hashem helped me when I called to Him in truth.

Yirmiyah 17:7: A person who has trust in Hashem is blessed. Call out to Hashem in truth.

25. Torah Was Given Only to the Jews

We have to realize something special: The Torah was given to us to use and to gain from it.

Many people have the privilege of gaining so much Torah, but they don't allow themselves to. Instead they allow themselves to become glued in *Olam Haze*. We glued ourselves in *Olam HaSheker*, the false of this world, but after 120 years, we are all going to leave this world to go to the Next World. We have to acquire the Next World, the World of Truth, the right way. We must attach ourselves to it by learning Torah and performing misvot.

Zeh haTorah shelanu, this is *our* Torah: This Torah is only for us; the more we gain Torah, the more we are attaching ourselves to the Master of the Universe.

May we all realize that the more Torah and misvot we do in this world, the more we are attaching ourselves to Hashem.

26. From the Heart

Mishlei 15:13 states, "A glad heart cheers the face."

When you are truly happy and know that Hashem is the One giving you everything, you'll be happy to give charity and help yeshiva and kollel students who learn Torah all their lives.

When you want to perform a good deed, let it come from the heart.

You truly want to give it; you truly want to give it from the heart.

One of my friends asked me a beautiful question. He asked, "If I am doing misvot but it's really not coming from the heart, should I continue performing them or should I stop?"

I quoted a Gemara (*Pesachim* 60a): Rabbi Yehuda said in the name of Rav, "A person is supposed to engage in misvot and Torah."

[Even if you are simply performing them and not doing them for the sake of Heaven or from the heart, you are supposed to do them.]

The Gemara continues, "Continue performing misvot and learning Torah, because sooner or later it'll come for the sake of Heaven and it will come from the heart."

Lev semichah yetiv: A happy heart will want to give because the person is happy with what he has.

Always do things from the heart.

27. Turn from Bad

It states in *Mishlei* 3:7, "Turn away from evil."

We have to try our best to always examine ourselves to discover the bad and stay away from the evil path.

Mesillat Yesharim, Chapter 2 says that we all have to be open to recognize our actions, whether they are bad or good.

When a person does a good deed in this world, it will give him or her the pleasure to want to do more good deeds in this world, and that will make the person turn away from bad.

It states in *Tehillim* 34:16, "Turn away from the bad and do good." We have to realize once you turn from evil, you will have the ability to do good. Rabbi Eli Mansour says on the words, "turn away from evil and do good," every single person should start doing good and then he or she will automatically not want to do bad.

The *Mesudat David* states that the *Mesillat Yesharim* comes to teach us that the direction of a person is to turn himself or herself from doing evil.

Direct yourself in the right path.

28. Who Will Help?

A few years ago, there was a young woman who got married and a few months later was divorced.

The woman was in pain for weeks and months. She was broken and was turned off from everything she saw. She did not want to do anything; nothing helped her. She wasn't interested in anything. The lady couldn't believe how her marriage had ended so quickly-

One day, she opened a *Sefer Tehillim* and started praying to Hashem nonstop. She kept praying until tears ran down her face. After reading the powerful words, she realized that Hashem had done the best thing for her and this was what was meant to happen. She realized that this was all the hand of Hashem guiding her through this world.

When I heard this story, I was shocked and I became inspired that a young woman could go through a test like this, and at first she was broken, but then she fought herself and realized and said to herself, "Who is going to help me? The help is going to come from Hashem."

Sometimes in life we ask ourselves questions: From where is the money going to come? How am I going to find my soulmate?

We have so many questions in life but once we will realize that Hashem is the King of everything, then we'll be much more relaxed and calmer with everything that comes our way in life.

I have the biggest privilege of having Rabbi David Ashear as my mentor, guiding me. Some of the ideas he speaks about I analyze and try to make everyone realize that there is Hashem in the world and yes, He wants to help us with everything we are going through in life.

"Hashem will always help you."

29. Learn the Torah with Compassion

We all shouldn't forget that the Torah was given to us only.

The Torah is something that each person should not forget and always remember the Torah and misvot: My son, don't forget the Torah!

We all should consider ourselves so lucky that we are the chosen nation and we were given the true, precious Torah that will make a person perfect in all his ways.

It states that with all our ways we should make the Torah a part of us. The more you learn Torah, the more you're going to see the hand of Hashem every day.

This incident happened to me and I saw Hashem's help directly. I was sitting with my *chavurta*, study partner, and we were both learning a *sugya*, topic, in Gemara: He was learning and I was learning and he was writing notes and I was writing notes: I didn't know what he was really learning but I knew he was learning.

I had a serious question on the topic we were learning and I was trying to find the *psak*, halachic decision. I was learning with passion and he was learning with full passion.

I looked up from my Gemara and asked him, "What is the *psak* on this? I'm having trouble finding it."

He looked at me in surprise, saying, "Eli, I'm also trying to find the *psak halacha*!"

This was directly Hashem's hand helping me to learn. The more you learn the Torah with a passion, the more you'll see Hashem's help.

Another incident happened the same day.

My *chavurta* asked one of the guys a question that he was having trouble with.

The person replied, "I am writing the answer to that question right now!" He did not know that my *chavruta* was going to ask him for help.

with that question, but Hashem knew!

This is why *Mishlei* tells us, "My son, don't forget," and that is the power of learning Torah with full passion.

30. Hashem Wants to Hear from You

Many people think negative thoughts about praying; they say, "I prayed to Hashem so many times to give me what I want, but Hashem isn't listening to my prayers." That's why many people give up on their prayers—because they don't recognize any results of their prayers. This is a false conclusion, and a person should not think like that.

Hashem wants to hear from you! Even if you don't get what you want, always have hope in Hashem and be strong, as the verse states, "Place your hope in Hashem."

Have hope that Hashem will protect you and give you what you truly need.

People should always have this in mind: Hashem knows what's best for you, better than you know.

A person should never think that prayers are useless. That's not true…. Prayer is the key to everything and Hashem does hear your *tefillot*, prayers.

Tehillim 7:10 tells us:

Hashem has heard my entreaty Hashem will accept my prayers.

We all should know that if we pray for something and don't see the result we wanted, we must have hope and go back and pray harder to Hashem.

31. Watch Your Ways

Mishlei 8:32 states, "My sons, listen and watch your ways."

This comes to teach us a lesson in life, which is stated in the next verse: Listen to *mussar*, reproof, and gain from it.

The *mussar* you hear is going to lead you to do good. Whenever you hear *mussar* on any topic, try to focus on the message; hear it and take the *mussar* on your own behalf and change your ways from the bad to the good.

The *Mesudat David* writes on the word *hear*: Hear the *mussar* of being a person who fears Hashem. The special trait of having fear of Hashem means that you won't come to sin.

Each person has an obligation to examine himself or herself to stay away from bad.

Mesillat Yesharim (Chapter 3) states that people have to be honest with themselves and examine their actions to see whether they are good or bad. We all have to be watchmen on ourselves to stay always from evil as much as possible. When you stay away from evil, you have the status of *tahor*, purity, which is holy.

We all have to listen to *mussar* and change our ways to go in the direction of Hashem. When you listen to *mussar* and change your ways, you'll be the happiest person.

In Arbit, we say these powerful words: We tell Hashem, Hashem, You are the King Who guards us from all the evil things.

Hashem is the One Who is going to protect you from all the evil things, but you must watch yourself and be careful with all your actions.

Those who hear the *mussar* that is really needed in their lives and they listen to it and they fix their ways, they are called praiseworthy:

Praiseworthy is a person who listens to the *mussar*.

When you gain from the *mussar* and changes your ways, you are praiseworthy in Hashem's eyes.

Watch your ways today.

32. The Power of Being Humble

The first words in the *Orchot Tsaddikim*, *Gate of Being Humble* start off by telling us that being humble is the greatest character trait.

The power of being humble is that for any good deeds you do with the trait of being humble, Hashem will reward that specific deed.

Yirmiyah 7:21 states that if someone has the trait of being humble, everything is going to be good.

Any time a person's day isn't going too well, he'll know how to deal with it, because that is the power of being humble.

A person should always be humble with his parents and his Rabbis.

Don't strive to be a big shot; rather, train yourself in being humble with anything you do in life.

A person being humble won't come to do the following things:

1. Get angry.
2. Come to sin.
3. Be a big shot.

Train yourself to be a person who is humble.

33. Prayers Is Your Medication

Many people fall into a sickness of feeling hopeless, feeling that no one is there for them, and no one is listening to their prayers, and they start doing things that they're not supposed to do.

If we would only know that the medication for all our problems is prayer! Prayer is the master medicine for all your issues, whether they are financial or personal needs. Spiritually turn to Hashem, because that is the best medicine for you.

When you are sick, of course you must put all your effort into becoming well, attending a good doctor and doing what the doctor tells you, but, of course, the end result is in Hashem's hands.

Parashat Mishpatim (21.19) states, "*V'rapo yerapeh*—and he shall heal."

Hashem is the only One Who has a time frame when you're going to be healed; you must turn yourself to Hashem in anything you're going through in life.

Prayer is the medicine for everything!

If you are looking for a job—turn to Hashem and pour your heart out! Speak to Hashem.

A short parable can help us understand this concept better and apply it to our daily lives:

A father tells his son, "If you need something, turn to me and ask me—don't be shy."

The same idea is with Hashem: Hashem wants to hear from you—just turn to Him and pray and pour out your heart to Him.

The more you will pray to Hashem, the more Hashem will come close to you.

It states in *Tehillim* 145:18, "Call out to Hashem and He'll be with you in truth."

We all should realize how lucky we are that we have *tefillot* and these *tefillot* are free of charge.

No need to travel, no credit card, nothing at all.

All you need to do is to call out to Him in truth.

34. Open Your Heart

Every day during the *Amidah*, we say these words to Hashem, "*P'tach libi b'toratecha*, Please open my heart to Your Torah."

You should realize that when you talk to Hashem and tell him to open your heart to His Torah, you have to *want* to open your heart to the Torah.

We should take these words to heart every time we say the words *open my heart to Your Torah*.

After these powerful words, we say, "Let me run after the good deeds and let me perform them."

The more you will open up heart to the Torah and perform misvot, Hashem will protect you from all the evil things that want to knock you out.

Hashem would not let it happen as we say the words, "All the evil that wants to attack me, don't allow to do so, and Hashem, You should ruin their plans and they should be cursed."

We all should realize the truth of life: The more we open our hearts to the Torah and perform good deeds, all evil will be destroyed.

In other words, the Torah and misvot are protection for you.

Open your heart to do good in the world.

35. If I Am Not for Myself, Who Will Be for Me?

It states in *Pirkei Avot* 1:14, "If I am not for myself, who will be for me?"

Some people look at many good people in the world who are learning and performing good deeds, and they say, "Ay, *Baruch Hashem*, look at them! They're doing great!" Then they think, "You know what, I am exempt from all these misvot." False! Rather, a person should look at others and gain *chizuk*, encouragement, from them.

After seeing people doing good, you have to make the move to do good in the world and employ all the great things in your daily life. If you're not for yourself, doing good deeds and learning, then who will do them for you? Nobody can.

People can help you learn and teach you how to do good deeds, but at the end you must make the move, telling yourself, "I want to do good in this world."

Each person has to employ these words in his or her life, knowing that no one else can do his or her part in this world.

You must do what's right in this world. If you know a person who always had a smile on his or her face and was always in a happy mood and suddenly one day that person wakes up and says, "I'm done! No more smiling, no more going to shul." You be the one to give him or her the needed *chizuk*. It's so important for you to give others *chizuk*—the person who is always smiling and happy gives other people hope in Hashem and they remain happy. That is the important of give others *chizuk*.

I was once speaking to a friend who had fallen into a depression. He said, "What's the purpose of life?"

I could see that he was really upset and I said to myself, "Ay, Hashem, help me say the proper words—I really want to help this person."

I pulled out a *sefer* called *Pirkei Avot* and I showed him the following mishna: If a person is not for himself, doing all the good, then who will do it?

I said, "Jack, Hashem loves you. You have to understand that this depression and this kind of talk is all the evil inclination, and this is all fake, trying to make you upset."

The mishna is talking to everyone out there; if you're doing something and you stop, no one else will do it. You must be yourself and keep going and do good deeds and learn Torah.

When you see people who are upset, it's your obligation to help them out—don't turn away.

When a person needs *chizuk*, give it to him or her with a smile.

36. The Second Yehi Ratzon in Berchot Hashachar

May it be Your will, Hashem, My G-d, G-d of my forefathers…. These words are something we have to say with a full passion, realizing that You Hashem save me today, and each and every day.

As soon as you say these words, think about all the things that Hashem should protect you from. We talk directly to Hashem and ask Him with these powerful words that He should protect us from all the evil things in the world.

Then we say, "Save us from the *yetzer hara*, from the power of the evil inclination that wants to harm everyone out there.

In this prayer, you will have the chance to say the words with a full passion of staying away from the evil inclination.

We ask Hashem to save us from an evil eye, from the hatred of people, and then, finally, from *Gehinom*.

Sometimes, when we say this paragraph in the morning, we fly through the words and we don't even realize what we're saying. If we would think logically and realize that sometime many things fall onto a person, we will look at the words we say in the morning and say the paragraph with a full passion and understanding of what we are saying.

Yehi Ratzon is a blessing for *you*—not for anybody else. When you say the blessing with a full passion, you are blessing yourself.

We all should strengthen ourselves and commit to saying these words the proper way.

Let us all understand the meaning of each word we say in our prayers.

37. A Good Heart

Many people have a good heart. Our sages tell us anybody who has a good heart will always want to help others and be there for their daily needs.

I heard about something that happened to my friend's grandfather, Miro Chalouh, *a"h*. At first when I heard it, I was shocked. Then I spoke to my friend to hear the whole story. He said I heard it already during the *arayat*.

Miro Chalouh *a"h* was the one opened up the Chalouh grocery store. Originally, he had a store in Syria, many years. At the *arayat* I heard a story about him that really gave me *chizuk*.

While still in Syria, Miro saw that there was a *levaya*, funeral, taking place. He quickly closed the store and went to fulfill the misva escorting the dead; this shows his good heart.

He cared about each person and always had a smile on his face no matter what happened to him. Years later. Miro and his children opened a grocery store in Brooklyn together. When I would go to that store, I always saw him giving people *chizuk*. His style of *chizuk* was telling everyone, "Taste before you buy!" In addition, he always used to smile at his customers.

He always spoke to people, telling them, "Don't worry, Hashem is in charge! Don't lose hope." A person like this was working and doing *avodat Hashem* at the same time.

Years passed and in the month of Adar in 2016, Miro was *niftar*, he passed away due to an illness. I heard Rabbi Shamah, the Rabbi of the Syrian shul in Brooklyn, Shevet Achim, give a powerful speech at the *arayat*, saying that when the doctors had to perform surgery and amputate his leg, Miro's reaction was lifting his eyes to Hashem and saying and feeling. "You, Hashem, know what you're doing and I accept whatever you're doing."

Days passed and this great person was *niftar*. Look at the actions of this simple person and how he took everything with love.

This man walked with Hashem all his life. Even during the days of suffering, he walked with Hashem and had hope.

We should always realize how great it is to live our lives with a good heart because when a person is in this world and walks with Hashem and does for others, that is the way he or she achieves greatness.

Have a *lev tov*, a good heart.

38. It's a Gift

Kohelet 3:11 states, "He [Hashem] had made everything beautiful in its time." Hashem made everything in life beautiful; even the bitter in it that seems bitter is still beautiful, since Hashem has a time frame and even if sometimes we look through our lives and say this is bad and this is bad and the list keeps going on, we have to realize that Hashem created the world in a beautiful fashion and we should consider it as the biggest gift.

Living in this world is the biggest gift and the question is why?

Why is it so special that each person is lucky and it is the biggest gift that we are alive?

The answer is in *Mesillat Yesharim*, Chapter 1: To earn *Olam Haba* we first need to enter this world of *Olam Ha'ze*.

The next *pasuk* in *Kohelet* states, "There's nothing better for them than to rejoice and do good in life."

Rashi says that there is nothing better for people than to rejoice in their lots and do what is right in G-d's eyes while they are alive.

Sometimes we live our lives full of complaints and becoming upset, and we say, "I want more of this, and I want this product, and why isn't the food better." The list of complaints goes on and all, of it simply negative.

If we think about it for a minute and realize how lucky we are that Hashem gave us so many good things in life, our mindset will change to the positive.

Pirkei Avot 4:1 states, "Who is rich? The one who is happy with what he or she has."

The person who is happy with what he or she has realizes that everything in life is the biggest gift from Hashem.

Everything that we see in our lives is a gift from the boss of the world—and that is Hashem.

Life is a gift.

39. Hashem Hears You

People face many problems in life, whether they are difficulties with money or issues in the home, such as having children, school problems, raising kids…the list goes on.

Every morning we say in the prayers of *Baruch She'amar*, "Blessed is he who decrees and fulfills." We should realize that whatever happens to us in life, we can't turn to anyone besides Hashem, because Hashem hears us and feels our pain. Turn only to Him and no one else.

Sometimes you see a person and things aren't going his way and he starts yelling and blaming himself. He falls into a trap, and that is a mistake of life. The only One to turn to is Hashem—He is the Master of everything and He is the only One Who has time for you.

Tehillim 24:16 states, "The eyes of Hashem are towards the righteous people and His ear are open to their cry." Hashem has the vision to know what's going on with us. With any problems that we face, Hashem is the only One Who can help us.

Hashem will never turn you down. *Tehillim* 24:17 states, Hashem hears, and from all their troubles, He saves them.

A person should always have this in mind: For anything you want in life, always tell yourself, "Hashem is hearing me"

In truth, Hashem does hear you.

40. Hashem's Plan

Many people in life make plans for everything. Some people make plans for one year from today, and some for two years, and some for three.

This can be good and this can be bad. It can be good because then you have an idea of what you want to become and how you want to manage. And it can be bad because sometimes in our lives we plan so many things and they don't go the way we want to; then we become angry and we lose our trust in G-d.

We should try our best to take life day by day, because at the end we have a King taking care of all our needs, whatever they are. Whether it's money, finding a soulmate, or anything else, G-d is the planner of everything.

We don't really plan anything; G-d is the Planner, as it says, "Many thoughts are in the heart of a man, but only G-d's counsel will stand forever."

G-d is planning everything; we should stop planning and focus on what we see today. Don't live for tomorrow's coming—live for today.

A person comes to the age of marrying. Some people ask themselves, "How can I get married? I have bills to pay, rent, school, and so on and so forth." That is why many people get afraid to get married; they think they need 100,000 dollars before they get married. That is false and that is the reason a person is supposed to live his life for what he sees today instead of thinking of what's going to happen in the future. First, get married and focus on the first year—why focus on what may happen ten years from now?

The truth is, this is all waste of time. When a person has the mindset of thinking what may happen 10 years from now, then that person is losing out. G-d has bigger plans than we do. Sometimes we think, "Only if I do this, and only if I have billions of dollars; I will give that organization," and so on!

Fool! G-d runs the world and He plans everything. G-d will never forget you or your prayers. Even if you plan and it doesn't go your way, be happy and live for today; as it says, "G-d won't cast off His people nor will He abandon His inheritance" (*Tehillim* 94:14.)

G-d planned your future, not you. Have trust Hashem and be patient with everything in life, because G-d plans.

41. Praise Hashem

Tehillim 146:2 states, "I will praise G-d as long as I live. I will sing to my God as long as I exist."

We should learn from David's attitude; all the time we are living in this world, we are supposed to praise G-d and show gratitude to G-d by saying, "G-d, thank You for giving me life, a lovely home, lovely parents, etc." For all the gifts that our Father gives us, we always have to praise and show gratitude to the only One.

The special secret is that if you thank God for whatever you are going through, G-d will shower you with blessing. Since G-d sees that you are suffering and you still show gratitude, G-d says, "You are still thanking Me; I must give you something good."

As long as you are living, you should always be praising G-d for all the kindness G-d has given you.

We all should realize the biggest gift for the life we have is praising G-d for everything He gives us.

You should be praising only G-d, nobody else. Of course, if someone does you a kindness, show the person gratitude and thank him or her for the action that was performed for you, but we should thank G-d for sending this messenger to help you out.

Do not place trust in people who have no power of deliverance.

G-d is the One Who will show us the salvation, and nobody else. The more you praise Hashem, the more you'll see the salvation.

42. Only Hashem Himself

Tehillim 92:1 states, "All will thank You."

We all should thank only Hashem Himself when we get our paycheck or when anything good comes our way. Thank Hashem alone because He is the One Who is giving you all the good.

A person who is giving you something good is a messenger from Hashem Who is allowing him to do so, and of course, a person is supposed to show gratitude to his fellow men.

Show gratitude to Hashem and to the people around you, because whatever you get you still have to thank Hashem and the person who gave you what you needed. "All will praise you."

As I write on the topic of praising, we should always praise Hashem for everything He does for us at every moment.

When you praise Hashem, that shows Hashem that you're praising him for everything you have. Whether it is bad or good, you still praise Him. Then Hashem looks at you and says, "Wow! I actually gave you an affliction and you still thanking Me and praising Me." Hashem says, "I will pay you with all the good."

We all have to remember that Hashem is the only One Who is helping you and guiding you.

43. Give It Up

When the Temple will be built, people will bring offerings for Hashem.

I heard a beautiful word from Rabbi Eli Mansour. He said that when the brothers, Kayin and Hevel, brought offerings, Hashem accepted Hevel's and not Kayin's.

Havel knew what kind of offering he should give to Hashem, while Kayin didn't know much.

We learn here a big secret in life: Even though Hashem did actually accept the offering from Hevel and not Kayin, Hevel still made a mistake by not telling Kayin what to do.

Every morning in our daily prayers, we say that we should learn and teach. The more you learn from your rabbi and share it with others, you are rewarded for every time you repeat the lesson.

When I was in Yeshivat Lev Aharon, I was told to speak in front of all the yeshiva students and rabbis. I didn't know what to say; I was speechless. Then I started to think deeply regarding the word *Korban*, Offering.

I starting speaking about a *Korban*, describing how people used to bring it to the Temple and burn it for Hashem. That was the way people became close to Hashem. Sometimes in life, when you want to do a kindness you have to sacrifice yourself by giving in. When you give in, that is giving up everything for Hashem.

The word *Korban* is related to the word *karov*, closeness. To get close to Hashem, you must offer yourself everything you have, you have to give in.

When you really want to walk in the ways of Hashem, you must tell yourself, "I am throwing away all the stupid things out there that are holding me back. I want to get close to Hashem!" In order to do that, you must give up on things you have.

The things you're addicted to, the things that you can't let go—those are the things that are blocking you from becoming close to Hashem.

To have clarity in life, you first have to remove all bad traits from yourself. Giving up on everything and learning and doing service of Hashem is the way to gain full protection. If you look at the word *le'lamad*, you shall learn that the numerical value is 104. That is the value of Hashem's Name four times.

If you build yourself up by learning something four times and Hashem's Name becomes part of you.

Why four times? Because a person gets home from work and he's tired. All of a sudden, he overcomes his test and goes to class: that's one time. Driving or walking to the class: that's two times. When he gets there, he opens the Gemara and starts learning: that is three times. When he finally learns it thoroughly and understands it: that's the fourth time, and that is completely fulfilling the word *le'lamad*.

To learn Torah and gain closeness to Hashem, you have to give up everything else and move a step further.

44. The Power of Saying Birkat Hamazon

Men and women have an obligation to recite *Birkat Hamazon* after they have a meal that includes bread.

Saying the blessing with the proper mindset and saying the words correctly will bring you the livelihood you're striving for.

We say the words, "Blessed are You, Hashem our G-d, King of the universe, Who feeds us."

G-d is the One taking care of us every single day of our lives. This is the power of saying this blessing that will gain you everything in life.

This world is full of kindness and compassion, as it states, with His goodness G-d gives and sustains every single being with food and with everything else; that is the great kindness of G-d.

As the words state, G-d gives bread to all mankind. We should look at the words and realize how powerful they are: G-d gives everything, including money. He provides for everybody—wealth and food and everything that man needs. Try your best to at least say these words with full understanding.

A person who wants money must see this blessing with the completely proper mindset. Likewise, if you sit down for a good twenty minutes to have an amazing meal, you must show gratitude to G-d by saying *Birkat Hamazon*. That is why we say the words, "we give thanks to You, G-d." We have to thank Hashem for everything.

A person who truly wants a good livelihood should say this blessing with the proper mindset, and he must believe that it's the truth.

This is the power of saying *Birkat Hamazon*.

45. The Power of Speech

The mouth of a person is a powerful tool in life, and we have to be careful with the way we speak to people, whether they are our parents, our friends, or anybody else. Even when you learn a new law in Judaism, you must express it in the proper way so that people won't get hurt and they'll understand it and follow it.

You can't speak to them in a harsh way; you have to say it with complete love.

Rabbi Yaakov Mizrachi from Jerusalem came and visited United States. He made a speech, and he mentioned that a person shouldn't even allow any negative words out of his mouth. Why? because Hashem is listening to you and the way you speak. As we see, when Moshe Rabbeinu told G-d, "Erase me from Your book," Hashem listened to him—you won't find the name of Moshe in *Parashat Tezaveh* since Moshe asked G-d to erase him from the Torah and not destroy Klal Yisrael. Hashem listened to the words that came from his mouth.

People live their lives saying words without thinking that if you're using your words and saying bad, G-d forbid, it will happen. Don't open your mouth to the evil. Never say to yourself comments such as, "Oh, I don't want to get married," because G-d hears you.

A. Satan hears you.
B. Rabbi Yaakov

Mizrachi told about a neighbor who was driving all day. The neighbor said something about his hands and all of a sudden, the next day, his hands blew up. This is why we have to be careful with the way we speak to people and also the way we speak to ourselves.

Words are more powerful than smacking someone in the face.

People will always remember the words you said. Let us all use our mouths to talk nicely with our friends, with our spouse, with our friends, with our workers, etc.

We should all use our mouths to speak only good.

46. Torah Is Life

It states in *Pirkei Avot* 2:8, "The more Torah you have, the more life you have."

The more a person engages himself with the Torah and learns, he gains life. The more you learn, the more you are alive.

You will see the truth in life: The more you learn, the more you are living your life to greatness.

When a person learns Torah, he'll have clarity in him; he'll have direction in his life.

Rabbi Ezra Dayan says, "A person without Torah is like a walking dead."

Torah itself is a protection for us, both physically and spiritually.

The Torah can destroy the evil inclination.

Masechet Kiddushin 30b states: The Gemara says anybody who is engaged in Torah will never be trapped by the evil inclination.

This is the power of studying Torah every day. Torah is oxygen for us; it keeps us going. Without it, we're dead.

The *Nefesh HaChaim* states:

Any person who is occupied with Torah studies, makes Hashem so happy. It's as if the world was recreated; Torah makes the world be born; without it the world is dead.

When you learn Torah, besides being the happiest person, you are also lighting up the world and you're lighting a special light inside of you. As it says, "A good deed is a candle and the Torah you learn is the light."

We are placed in this world to toil in Torah and misvot as much as we can (*Mesillat Yesharim*).

Mishna Peah 1 states: Torah beats all other great deeds. Torah is equivalent to all the mitzvos.

Learning Torah is one of the greatest misvot of the 613 misvot.

You're building your own Heaven by sitting down and learning Hashem's Torah.

Pirkei Avot 2:8 tells us, "Acquire words of Torah and you'll acquire Heaven."

Let us all be attached to Torah as much as we can.

47. Stay Away from a Bad Friend

It states in *Pirkei Avot* 2:14: Go out and go see which bad direction you should stay away from. Rabbi Yehoshua says, A bad friend."

Our sages tell us a person should always stay away from bad friends. Why? Because if a person is going to be around bad friends and socialize with them, he will end up doing what they're doing, such as cursing, disrespecting people, smoking, and other bad things.

A person who wants to learn Torah and become close to G-d has to first get rid of all his bad friends and all the bad characters. Avoiding the bad is the key. When a person stays away from bad friends, he'll return to G-d and reach the highest spiritual level.

Don't socialize with bad friends. Don't blind yourself to the evil that wants to destroy you and make you further from G-d. Stay away from bad friends today and start learning Torah. When you learn the Torah, you will automatically feel complete and all your sins that you did are erased.

The *Nefesh HaChaim* writes that when you learn the Torah, all your sins are forgiven.

48. Start Now

People grow up with the attitude, "Right now, I want to live my life the way I want it and do things how I want."

People ask others, "When are you planning to start learning Torah and go in the right path?"

They respond, "Nah, I still have a long time; I want to live my life first." That is the biggest mistake people make; they have to fix their way of life.

It states in *Pirkei Avot* 1:14, "If not now, then when?"

If you are not going to do the service of Hashem today, then when are you going to start? You all have to start now in learning; you all have to start now to look at your ways and see if they are good or bad.

The more you learn Torah, the more you are building up the world.

Without Torah learning, the world is nothing; it is full of emptiness.

Torah makes people happy. Torah makes everything better. We all have to start today to place ourselves in a good environment.

Pirkei Avot 2:8 states that the more Torah you have, the more life you have.

It's never too late to start. There's always time to grow in Hashem's ways and become who you are really supposed to be.

Start now.

49. Stay Away from Bad

It states in *Devarim* 23:10, "A person should watch himself from doing any bad."

We have an obligation to avoid bad, whether we are men, women, or even kids. Parents should train their kids when they are young to stay away from bad and from all the garbage technology out there that wants to destroy us.

Parents have to ask where their kids are going and find out to whom they are talking?

We all have an obligation to try to fix the world by bringing people closer to Hashem. We can't be selfish and look out only for ourselves; we must look out for others and try to help them. Many people are jobless and wandering in the streets. Be that person who helps; don't be that person talking negatively. Be that person to help him and support him.

I always ask myself, *Why is all this happening?*

I thought about it really hard and deep: It's because it people are okay with giving young children technology and all the garbage out there and think their kids are doing good. No, this is false. We all have an obligation to helping people in every way.

I once heard Rabbi Ephraim Waxman saying that parents that give their children a phone with access to the internet is like giving them a loaded gun.

Where are our brains?

We all have to think for a moment and ask ourselves: Wait! What am I doing giving my six-year-old child an iPhone that has internet?

Is it fair to give a children technology and not care what they do with it?

I have seen a three-year-old girl holding an iPhone in her hands and her mother seemed okay with it. I said, "Oh, my goodness!" All of a sudden, the mother was asking permission from the daughter, saying, "I need the phone." The mother grabbed it and the daughter started to cry as if something happened, Heaven forbid.

I looked at this child and said to myself, "*Ay*, Hashem! It has gone this far that kids are at the age of 3 are holding an iPhone and the question is who's the one giving it to whom?"

Sad to say, it's the parents' faults and they are okay with it. That is the biggest mistake and we all have to fix it by not giving garbage to our kids.

The Torah says we all should stay away from evil today.

50. The Spark Is in You

Every Jew has a special spark in him or her. To make the spark light up, we have to work on ourselves.

Hashem placed a soul in every single human being. Without that soul, we don't have any flesh; we are nothing. Without the soul, there's no existence.

How lucky we are and blessed that we have a soul and we can make that soul light up and keep it lighting. The way to make the spark light in us is by learning the Torah that Hashem gave us.

Are we going to take that spark and light it or we going to make it dark?

Mishlei 6:23 states, "The Torah is the light." Torah is what makes a person's spark light.

To light the spark, we have to toil in Torah.

51. Torah Erases Your Sins

It states in the *Sefer Nefesh HaChaim*, "A person who is engaged in Torah, the Torah learning will merit your forgiveness for all the sins you committed in the past."

When you go to a learning program to learn and to become a better person, all the bad deeds you did will be forgiven.

That is the power of Torah Torah is holy and whenever something is so holy, it will automatically erase all the bad deeds.

The *Nefesh HaChaim* writes, "A person who is engaged in Torah will have a pure mindset and clarity of thought."

The biggest investment to do is listening to these words by learning Torah. When you learn Torah, all your sins are erased. That is the powerful of learning Torah.

People who learn Torah will gain so many good benefits, such as:

1. Seeing Hashem in his life
2. Being happy
3. Having clarity
4. Being holy.

Learning Torah will erase your sins.

52. You Won't Come to Sin

People who want to stop sinning should keep three things in mind: *Pirkei Avot* 2:1 tells us:

Know three things and you won't come to sin. Know what is above you:

1. An Eye that see everything
2. An Ear that hears everything
3. All your actions, good or bad, are written in a Book.

The first one: Know that Hashem is above you and is clearly watching you. When you know that Hashem is watching, you won't come to sin.

People can tell themselves, "It's dark; nobody can see me. I will commit a sin nobody is looking at me," No, you fool! Hashem is watching you at all times. All your actions that you do, Hashem sees and He hears what you tell yourself.

We all have to study this concept and ingrain it in our hearts and minds.

The first thing we have to know is to know what is above us and the second is to know that Somebody is looking at us and He is listening at us at all times and all the things we do in this world are written in His Book.

All your actions are written in the Book.

53. The Power of Strength

We say in the morning blessings, "Blessed are You, Hashem, Who gave us strength."

Many people use their strength to do wrong things, such as running to do bad and running to violate people. One of the biggest mistakes people make is taking the power that Hashem gave us and using it the wrong way.

One reason we have strength is to perform the service of Hashem; that is the correct way to use our strength.

The *Mesillat Yesharim* writes that people are created to toil in Torah and to become a better people.

To become a better person, you must do something to yourself by learning Torah and performing misvot.

Never tell yourself that you don't want to use your strength in learning; rather, you'll just use it to doing the wrong things.

We all must realize the great power we have is because Hashem giving us the power.

54. Ask for Knowledge

Many people are seeking to be smart in learning, work, school, and everything else that people touch. They want to be smart in things they want to do, which is the greatest thing a person can achieve.

Hashem gives each person a specific thing that he or she can do, and some don't have the same abilities, but each person has to remember one thing: In anything you do, you need knowledge to know how to do things. In the *Amidah*, we say the words, "You (Hashem) favor men with perception and teach mankind understanding."

Hashem gave each person perception; that is the understanding to understand things. Others say that perception tells you what to do.

We all have the amazing privilege to take this prayer more seriously. Everyone in life wants to be successful in learning, work, school—there's a solution for that, and that is praying this blessing with a full passion: You favored each person with understanding.

We pray that Hashem grant us with wisdom, understanding, and knowledge. For you to have all these, you must first pray for them. You say the word wisdom, and Hashem gives you wisdom. You need wisdom and when you'll need wisdom, you'll have it. Wisdom is understanding: understanding the Gemara's questions and answers, understanding what to do at work, etc. Once you have full understanding, you'll have knowledge—the knowledge to know things.

You first must pray for it. Many time people say, "I want," but before you say the words, "I want," say the word, "I should pray for it."

We all have to train our minds to tell ourselves that when we need anything in life, we have to know one thing, and that is to pray for it.

Prayer is the master key for all problems.

Do you want knowledge? All you have to do is ask for it. Hashem is ready for you when you're ready to ask for it.

55. Come Back

If, Heaven forbid, you commit a sin, don't allow the evil inclination to overtake you and tell you that you're a loser and you just sinned, so how can you learn Torah?

Don't listen to anything and come back to Hashem. If you did fall, get back up and fight the battle!

It's not about how hard you fall; it's about how hard you're going to get back up.

We all fall into sins, we all make mistakes in life, but the main thing we should have in mind is to come back to Hashem.

People are born with tests and these tests that we face are meant to make us great.

We say in the *Amidah*, "Bring us back, our Father, to toil in Your Torah." We ask Hashem, "Hashem, bring us back to Your holy Torah."

Why? Because even if we fall and do the worst things, we can still ask our Father, "Hashem, bring me closer to your Torah."

Come back to Hashem! Even if you did sin, come back to Hashem and start learning Torah.

Don't look back at what you did; look at the next thing you can do: Become closer to Hashem.

To become closer to Hashem, admit to Hashem, "I sinned and I want to come back to You."

56. Don't Panic

Sometimes in life we face challenges; some are hard or some are easy. Sometimes when people face a challenge or something strange happens, they start to panic and get worried.

Hold off—take a deep breath and realize that there is a solution for everything. The first thing we have to know is that Hashem is the One Who decrees and fulfills.

We have to understand a major concept in life: Anything that happens to you is decreed from Hashem and He is doing it for your best.

I once heard from Rabbi Eliezer Ginsberg, "A person cannot stub a toe unless it was decreed from *Shamayim*."

We all should realize that Hashem is the Master of all plans and He is the only One Who can help us.

When you are driving, and you get into traffic, don't get frustrated and start yelling. Rather, be calm and talk to Hashem to help you.

There's no need to yell.

Everything that happens is decreed from Hashem, and anything that you see is a test for you to become better.

This happened to a friend of mine:

He lost his jacket in yeshiva and he started to panic. I ran over to him, telling him, "Saul, calm down and say this prayer and give charity.

With Hashem's help, you'll get it back."

A few days passed and he found his jacket. He realized that someone had borrowed his jacket without telling him.

We learn a powerful thing from this incident:

Whatever happens, you can't panic; you have to remain calm and pray to Hashem. When you have trust in Hashem, you'll never come to panic. Don't panic.

57. Hashem's Power

Hashem is the only One Who had the power to create the whole world within six days and made Shabbat for a rest day on which no work can be done.

Shabbat is the day of rest, to learn Torah and be with the family.

Hashem has the power to do anything. He is the One Who sustains us with money, food, and everything else. Hashem is the Boss.

Sometimes in life we face difficulties and we just want to give up and not want to do good anymore. That is a mistake; we should view all of our afflictions as:

A. As a wake-up call—Hashem is trying to wake you up to do *teshuva*.
B. It's a test—Hashem wants you to accept it with love. The Dubno Maggid relates the following parable:

A poor person was walking on the road, carrying a heavy bag. He was struggling along when suddenly a wealthy person passed by in a carriage.

He said to the poor man, "Come, I will take you where you want to go." The poor looked up in amazement, and asked, "You can take me?"

The wealthy person said, "Yes, come!"

The poor man climbed into the carriage and placed his heavy bag on his lap. The wealthy person noticed this and said, "What are you doing? Place the bag on the floor."

The poor man answers, "It's enough that you are taking me, you don't have to carry my bag as well."

The wealthy man replies, "Put it down; it's the carriage that's taking both us and our baggage." What do we learn from this parable?

Sometimes in life we take so many things on ourselves and we think we are in charge. Don't be a fool; stop holding on to your problems. Let them go and Hashem will carry them for you!

With any problem you face, instead of taking it and fighting yourself, allow Hashem to fight it for you, because he is the One Who is taking care of it—not you. Hashem is in charge—not you.

When you are getting married and you first start looking for an apartment, before you look—talk to Hashem and ask Him, "Hashem, please help me find something good," because He is the One Who is going to help you.

When anything that happens to you, don't blame yourself and don't blame others. Turn to Hashem and speak to Him for help because He has the power to help you.

Everyone should have a vision in their lives and understand the concept that it's Hashem Who makes a decree upon a person, not anybody else. Hashem is the One Who cures everyone.

He is the One Who wants to help you, but first you must call out to Him.

58. Danger of Lashon Hara #2

Alert! Don't allow your mouth to speak evil!

The Chofetz Chaim says: When you speak *lashon hara*, you are destroying the world and destroying the person that you're talking about.

We all have to be aware of how we speak to people. Speech is very powerful, more powerful than hitting someone. Words are never forgotten.

When you see something that doesn't look right, don't allow yourself to think, "Wow, this person is so bad!" You don't know what happened, so you must judge favorably and not speak bad about that person.

The Chofetz Chaim says when someone speaks *lashon hara*, the Gates of Prayer are closed. In order to open the Gates of Prayer, you must watch the way you speak to and about people.

Tehillim 34:13 states, "Who is the man who desires life? Who loves days of good?" David HaMelech says, "Guard your mouth from evil and your lips from talking bad."

Many people go out to rabbis to get a blessing for money, health, finding a shidduch, etc. The power of blessing is to watch your mouth and not to speak *lashon hara*—that is the blessing: to remain quiet.

It is recommended to buy a *sefer* of the *Daily Chofetz Chaim* to read every day

59. Being Patient

Our sages tell us that each and every human being needs the character trait of being patient. Why?

A person who wants to get married must be very patient and pray to Hashem for results. The value that a person gains from being patient is knowing that Hashem is in charge. The person knows that whatever happens to him, Hashem is the One taking care of everything.

When a person thinks that he's running the show and he's the one who is taking control of everything, we call this person a big fool because he doesn't realize that Hashem is taking care of him.

When you're stuck in traffic instead of yelling and going crazy, be patient and talk to Hashem and He'll help you. Just speak to him; pour out your heart to Him, because He wants to help you! When you are in any situation where you're waiting for something, be patient. Open a Tehillim and read the psalms.

My mother-in-law, Shella Yaich, Hashem should bless her, told me she was once stuck in traffic, and the cars weren't moving. She grabbed a *Sefer Tehillim* and said a few chapters. Suddenly the traffic cleared. The point is that she remained calm and prayed to Hashem, and Hashem helped her.

Be patient today and Hashem will calmly be with you.

60. Pray in Shul

The Gemara (*Berachot* 6a) states, "No prayer is answered until you pray in a shul." Why does it say this?

The Gemara answers: To find Hashem, you need ten men to form a minyan, and that is in shul, and that is where your prayers will be answered.

Your prayers will be heard in a shul. Everyone must try his best to always pray in shul with a minyan; that is where the *Shechina* rests—when there are ten people praying together. The power of praying in a shul with ten people is that you'll be successful in anything you do since Hashem is there hearing you.

We have no excuse to say, "Shul is too far." *Baruch Hashem*, there are many shuls out there. It's up to you to get up and go to shul, because when you walk to shul you are walking to Hashem's house.

A short parable will illustrate the idea.

A king owns a huge palace and tells all the people in the kingdom, "Whenever you need something, all you need to do is come to the palace and ask me for whatever you want and I will give you the things you need."

So, too, Hashem: His palace is the shul where you go to pray to Him and tell Him what you need.

If you want your prayers to be heard, go to a shul and pray with a minyan, because the King Who owns that palace is Hashem, and He has all types of gifts that He wants to give you.

Many people, unfortunately, come to shul and hang out and talk during prayers. Hashem does not want that from you; He wants you to come and pray to Him. The shul is a place for us to gather together and pray.

A shul is not meant for talking; it was built for us to pray to Hashem.

61. What's the Real Medicine?

Many people fall into a depression and have anxiety. They start going to doctors and they take medication and that is all lack of *emuna*, trust in Hashem.

When you study the concept of having trust in Hashem, you will never come into this trap of depression or anxiety.

The question is, what is the real medication we should take?

Mishlei 3:8 states, "The Torah is a healing for the body itself in this world and in the world to come."

The next time you fall into a depression, ask yourself why you are depressed; the answer is that you don't have the truth in you, and that is the Torah.

One day I asked Rabbi Yaakov Kalmanowitz, "Rabbi, how are you feeling?"

He responded, "*Baruch Hashem*, I'm feeling good. Torah is helping me; it's curing me."

The concept of learning Torah will protect you. That is why we say the Torah of Hashem is perfect: Because when you learn it, you'll be perfectly safe from all sorrows.

Learn the Torah today.

62. Fear Hashem

The Gemara in *Berachot* 6b states that if a person who has in him the fear of God, Hashem will listen to all his words.

Why?

Because when a person fears Hashem, Hashem says, "Wow, he's fearing Me. I would love to hear what he has to say." It's like a father and son: the son is scared of his father and the father wants to hear from his son.

The Gemara says that the world was created all for men to have fear of Hashem. The benefit of having fear is that Hashem is hearing your prayers and Hashem will be there for you and you won't come to sin.

We all have to remind ourselves that there's Someone watching us— and that is Hashem.

63. Learn from the Tiniest Thing

We have to view life knowing that everything was created by Hashem.

If you are having money troubles, turn to Hashem and pour out your heart. Have hope in Hashem because Hashem feels your pain. Put in your effort and pray to Hashem to help you.

The tiniest thing happened to me from which even till today I get so much *chizuk*. I walked into the bathroom and came out. I saw the whole vessel was full with water. That is the gift of Hashem. I gain much from that small thing.

We all have to look at the tiniest things and grow better because of them. We never should give up; we all have bumpy roads but they are all wake-up calls.

Learn from small things

64. Love Hashem

The *Pele Yoetz* brings down the power of loving Hashem, stating that there is no greater trait than to have love for Hashem. When you love Hashem, it'll make you come to wanting to do good deeds.

There's a rule in the Torah to love Hashem with all our hearts. That means giving up everything for the love of Hashem.

If you take the numerical value of the word *love* in Hebrew and double it, the number will be 26, which is the value of Hashem's Name.

Whenever you have love, Hashem comes into the picture.

When two people love each other, they are both having Hashem with them.

65. Pure Mindset

It states in *Tehillim* that Hashem created every human being with a holy heart, and a person must watch himself to stay away from sin.

In order for a person to see Hashem in his life, he must have a pure mindset. To achieve that is to train himself to always learn the Torah.

We all have a heart to want to do good in the world and some bad.

Every time you do bad, you're making your vision blurry and you won't be able to see the great things Hashem does.

To have a pure mindset, you'll have to work for it; that is done by learning the Torah and staying away from evil.

To stay connected with Hashem, you first have to remain pure; that means staying away from bad.

Make your view in life clear, not blurry.

The more we learn and fix our deeds, the more we make our minds pure.

66. Toiling Is What Counts

Many people find that when they sit down to learn Torah or they try to do a chesed, it's very hard for them, but the main thing is the toiling. The main thing is that you tried your best in doing, and that is what counts. When you toil, it's as if you actually did it.

When you don't understand something, don't tell yourself that you can't do it. That is not the solution; the solution is toiling again and again until you understand because Hashem wants you to be trying and toiling.

Hashem wants you to toil; that's all He want is you toiling, because that's what counts

67. Hashem's Mercy

Many of us fall in all kinds of different sins. Each person has his own challenge. Some are hard, some average, and some easy to overcome.

When you commit a sin, you should know you could come back to Hashem in instant.

Never tell yourself, "I give up! I sinned and Hashem hates me." That is all the evil inclination talking to you!

Hashem loves you and has mercy on you, just liked a father to a child. Hashem always has mercy on you. You should just have mercy on yourself by not committing sins.

Don't give up! Tell Hashem, "I'm sorry." That is the way to get back to Him because He has mercy and loves you.

I will conclude with a short parable:

The king told his slaves to work, but one slave didn't listen. The king took him by the neck and killed him. This is called *no mercy*!

Hashem looks at us and sees that we sin. We don't do the good things but He still has mercy on us because He loves us and cares about us.

Hashem isn't that king who wants to kill; Hashem is the One Who has mercy and love.

68. Look at Yourself

Don't look at others and say, "Because he is doing something wrong, I am going to do it, too. Because he talks in shul, I'm going to talk in shul, too." False! You should not look at others but rather you should look at yourself and fix yourself.

People go to weddings and tell themselves, "Wow, if that was my wedding, I would've spend another 100K." For what?!

Why impress people by trying to become better? If you truly want it, then it's a different story, but if you're doing it because you want to impress others, then you need help—because that's wrong.

When you see people who are going on vacation, don't tell yourself, "They are going, so I have to go." Many people fall into this mistake and they force their husbands to go on a 20,000-dollar vacation.

Why? Because they're looking at other people.

I once saw a boy who was on his phone while the rabbi was trying to make a speech. I went up to this boy and said, "Listen, please get off your phone."

He looked at me, saying, "Look, that guy is on his phone, so why can't I be on mine?" This is one of the biggest mistakes we all go make by looking at others and not looking at ourselves.

We know the Torah states that a person is not allowed to be jealous; the only time it permitted is when you see someone learning Torah and performing good deeds and you are jealous so you try to copy their deeds.

Don't look at others who are doing bad; look at people who are doing good.

69. Where Are You Headed?

Pirkei Avot 2:19 states, "Know Who is in front of you while you are toiling."

Each of you on your own level should ask yourself a question: Where I'm I headed?

Are you heading towards greatness or towards evil?

The only one who can answer that is you, yourself. Nobody knows the answer besides you.

For Whom is a person toiling?

The answer is you should toil in Torah for Hashem and nobody else.

Many people toil in Torah expecting things in return, and that is one of the biggest mistakes we have to avoid.

The Gemara in *Berachot* 17a states, "Praiseworthy is a person who toils in Torah."

When you learn Torah, you are praiseworthy in Hashem's eyes.

The garbage that is out there in the world is to make us further away from Hashem.

Everyone needs to toil in this world in order to enter Heaven.

While you are in this world, you are supposed to work hard to become a better person.

Ask yourself: Where am I headed in life?

70. It's About Love

Our sages tell us that the trait of love is a very strong tool in life and for everything out there.

When you want to do something in life, you first want to love it. If you don't love what you're doing, you'll feel miserable all the days. If you live, you must love what you're doing, no matter what.

To be happy, a person has to ask, "What do I have to do to make myself happy?" You have to answer that question; no one else can. You have to see what you love doing and stick to it.

When you do an action, it's because you love it. Whether it's praying, eating, physicality, or spirituality—it's because you love it.

Love brings you to want to do things in life.

Loves bring people closer to Hashem. To bring people to love Torah, you have to give in by loving them and giving them *chizuk*.

Everything needs love:

Marriage
Raising kids
Your job

Love is a great trait. The *Orchot Tsaddikim* writes in the *Gates of Love* that there two ways to look at love: It can be good or bad.

Good: Doing good deeds in this world because you love it.

Bad: You love to do bad, which is a big mistake.

Love what brings you connected to Hashem; without love you have no connection.

Love Hashem and love your fellow Jews.

71. The Real Vision

The real vision of life is to realize that we are in this world for a purpose: Not to do things we shouldn't be doing, but rather to toil in Torah and perform good deeds.

Each person's real vision is to toil in Torah and perform good deeds as much as he can.

Real vision is to realize how great Hashem is and how much He gave you. All the great things He gave you is because He loves you.

The real vision is to look at all the positive things you do and not the negative. When a person looks at this world as all a gift, that is a real vision.

Before you commit a sin ask yourself: What is it going to do for me? You will derive short-term pleasure—and then what?

You are going to feel like a piece of garbage!

Have a clear vision in your life by seeing the truth.

Look at the good side, not the bad.

72. Regret the Bad, Not the Good

Orchot Tsaddikim writes in the *Gates of Regret* that when you commit a sin and you have regret, that is repenting. Because you are feeling bad about it, your sin is forgiven.

When you commit a sin and you show Hashem that you regret it, Hashem automatically forgives you.

You should always regret the bad, but never regret the good. The good that you do, you should never regret.

Never tell yourself, for example, "I wish that I had never given charity." That is regretting the good, which is among the worst things to do. If you regret the good you've done, it's has if you never did those good deeds.

You can't tell yourself, "I will commit a sin and I will regret it later on." This is forbidden; you're not allowed to think like that. If you sinned and you have regret, that sin is forgiven, but you cannot tell yourself that you will sin and then come back. Never regret the good, but rather regret the bad.

73. The Power of Embarrassment

There are two types of embarrassment:

1. Embarrassing your friend.
2. Being embarrassed to do good for Hashem.

Many people live their lives being embarrassed to do things that they should be doing, such as wearing a kippa. Some people say, "I can't wear this, because if they see I am Jewish, they won't buy from me. I don't want them to know that I am Jewish." You should not have such ideas in your mind.

Don't be embarrassed to do good, because the good you do is going to get you into Heaven.

When a person is in an airport and there's minyan, instead of saying, "Oh, how am I going to pray; people will see me. I am not going to pray." You fool! Look at the Arabs—they hold a prayer rug all the time and when it is time for prayers, they start praying. This is how it should be, not caring about others and performing good deeds.

When a person is in shul and the minyan is praying, be embarrassed not to pray. Don't talk in shul. Don't talk during the reading of the *Sefer Torah*. Hashem is in front of you and doesn't want you to talk because it's Hashem's house.

A person should be embarrassed to do the following

1. Doing a sin
2. Cursing or disrespectful your parents
3. Talking in shul while praying
4. Embarrassing your friend

The Gemara (*Bava Metzia*) states, "A person who embarrasses his friend in public has no share in the World to Come."

We all have to avoid embarrassing anyone or speaking bad about anyone.

74. A Smile Can Change Your Day

Sometimes in life we face a challenge that is difficult, whether it's finding a job or finding a shidduch, and the list goes on...

The most important is a person wanting to do all these things must have that smile on his face.

Once a person has that smile on his face, that smile can change your whole day.

With anything you go through in life, always have in mind that it's all for the best. Say it with a smile, because a smile will change your outlook on life.

You always have to have a smile on you at all times. Chazal tell us that if someone is walking in the street and sees his friend, and his friend smiles and says hi, if the first one doesn't respond, he's a stealer.

The power of being happy and having that smile will change your day.

75. Clean Mindset

In *Tehillim*, David HaMelech says, "A heart that is pure Hashem created within me." When you train yourself not to look at things you shouldn't look at, that is how you keep your heart pure. But looking at things you're not supposed to is how you make your heart impure.

In order to put Torah inside you, you first must get rid of all the garbage that you have there.

The Gemara (*Berachot* 5a) states that each person should allow his good inclination to fight his evil inclination.

Each of us has a *yetzer hatov* and a *yetzer hara*. It is most important to allow the *yetzer hatov* to fight the *yetzer hara*; even if you fall, get back up and fight till you get it right.

Rabbi Ezra Dayan told me that by fighting the *yetzer hara*, you are a winner!

One day I was sitting with my chavruta and talking about the *yetzer hara*, and he told me a powerful point on how to look at it:

Two people are wrestling in a ring. John knocks out Steve, and Steve falls down. The referee starts counting to 10. He gets up to 7 and Steve gets up. This keeps on happening.

That is the way we have to view life: If we fall, the main idea is to get back up and fight the battle.

Don't place yourself in any test and that is the way you will remain pure.

76. How to Gain Purity

To really gain purity and to make your house pure, you will first need to know how to have a pure mindset and choose a direction that you know will not make you have any dirty thoughts, as what I wrote in the previous topic (Clean Mindset, above),

Question: How can a person gain purity for both himself and his household?

Mesillat Yesharim's chapter on purity states, learning Torah every day of your life is the way you'll have purity both in the home and in yourself.

Any person who has no Torah in himself is lost and is not pure at all! You must have Torah.

When your Torah studies are a part of you, you'll have a direction in life.

77. Hashem Is with a Tsaddik

The Zohar writes, "Hashem is with a righteous person in all his ways."

If you obey the Torah and misvot you are considered a *tsaddik*.

Hashem is watching you at all times, and whatever you do in life, Hashem is with you.

When you pray three times a day and learn day and night, you're a *tsaddik*. You should be proud of what you're doing.

Becoming a *tsaddik* takes time, but if you set goals for yourself, you'll get there

78. Engage in Torah

In *Parashat Tzav*, the *Zohar* states that any person who is engaged in Torah and his mouth speaks words of Torah, Hashem is sitting with him.

When you put yourself into a learning program, know that Hashem is with you—He is sitting near you.

The Zohar writes that the *Shechina* rests upon anyone who learns the Torah. The Torah is upholding the world; without it the world would be destroyed.

It's never too late to start learning Hashem's Torah. Hashem's Torah is so sweet that every time you learn it, you want to know more Torah. That is the power of engaging in Torah.

Learn Torah because Torah is what will make you enter Heaven. Two secrets I want to share:

1. When you learn Torah it as if you did *teshuvah*.
2. You are gaining *Olam Haba*.

79. Do It for Hashem

After 120 years in this world, we're all going to be judged on everything we did in this world.

Hashem is going to ask us many questions. One of the questions will be: Did you have time to sit down and learn My Torah?

When Hashem sends people to you to ask you when you are going to start coming to class, don't avoid them. Consider that a call from Hashem because He wants you to come to learn Torah.

If you are still sleeping, wake up, you fool! People think that they will be living in this world forever—that is false! Who knows what's going to happen tomorrow? Today, start doing things for Hashem, nobody else. Don't do it for anybody else; do it for your sake and for the sake of Hashem so that He will reward you.

I have to point out that we do live in a world that there are so many things that pull us away from learning. That is all the *yetzer hara* that always tries to pull us away and not wanting us to do good.

All the deeds that you do in this world should always be for sake of Hashem and nobody else.

The more you do things for Hashem, the more you are earning *Olam Haba*.

80. Pirkei Avot

The Mishna in *Pirkei Avot* will help the people aim for the truth and know how to live. Chapter 2, verse 13 states:

Go out and see what is good path to which you should attach yourself.

Rabbi Eliezer says, a good eye.

A person should be with friends who have a good eye. That means that every time they see you, they'll give you a nice compliment on how you look and make you feel happy. That is a good eye, because when people stare at you either they want to say something bad or good. That is why Rabbi Eliezer says attach yourself to friends who have a good eye.

Rabbi Yeshua says, a good friend.

It is important to have a good friend all the time, since whatever you do your friend will always help you and give you as much *chizuk* as you need. That is a good friend who will take care of you.

A person should always seek the truth and you should always be around people who have a good eye. That is a blessing, since they see you and they start giving you compliments to make you happy.

A person is considered a good friend because he is making you happy.

81. The True Desire

Mishlei 11:23 states that righteous people always desire to do good in this world. That is what we have to train ourselves to desire: misvot and learning Torah.

The *Mesudat David* writes that desire is a person desiring to do good.

There is a true desire and there is a false desire. A *tsaddik* will always say, "How can I help? What do you want me to do?" He is always looking forward to doing more. Whereas a *rasha* always desires to do bad in this world. That is why evil people are always unhappy with themselves.

Let us all work on ourselves to reach the desire of greatness.

82. A Tsaddik Is Like a Tree

It states in *Mishlei* 11:30, "The righteous people are like fruits."

The tree of life: The *tsaddikim* are compared to a big tree that grows fruits. Those fruits are *tsaddikim* that love the Torah so much it as if someone plucks out a ripe apple and bites on it. That's how *tsaddikim* are with Torah. The love that they have for the Torah is unbelievable.

When you perform misvot in this world, you don't know the benefit of what you are doing. It's as if a tree is growing full of fruits.

When people see that we are go in the path of Hashem, that will make them want to go in the proper path of life also.

A tree is a pillar of the fruits; it's the foundation. That is how a *tsaddik* is a tree that produces *tsaddikim*.

It is the greatest thing to know that a *tsaddik* is living for the truth.

83. Who's Really Going to Heal Me?

Many people have these words on their lips: I go to so many doctors and I'm still not feeling well.

Doctors are messengers of Hashem who are here to heal us and give us the right medicine.

You have an obligation to go to a doctor every time you feel sick and you must listen to what the doctors say. That is doing *hishtadlut*, putting in the proper effort. That effort is going to a doctor and taking the medicine he prescribes. At the end, Hashem will cure you; it's all up to Hashem.

The question is, who is really healing? Is it the pills? Is it the doctor?

The answer is, Hashem alone is helping you.

In the *Amidah* we say, "Heal us, Hashem." Hashem is the One and Only Who is going to heal you. You can go to the best doctors out there but the end result is that it's up to Hashem to heal you. That is why you always have to be close to Hashem with everything you do in life, because the end result is up to Hashem.

In the Amidah, when we ask Hashem to heal us, we're asking Him to heal us physically and spiritually.

Let us all remember one thing that it's Hashem alone healing us—nobody else.

84. Bitachon Is the Source of Everything

In the *Chovot HaLevavot's Gate of Trusting in Hashem*, the Lev Tov writes, to serve Hashem a person needs trust. You have to trust in Hashem with everything. Whatever He does, He is doing because it is best for you.

The Lev Tov writes something very interesting: Just as a slave has an obligation to serve his master and trusts his master, so too, we have Hashem Who runs the world as our Master, and we have to place our trust in Hashem and remain calm with everything in life, no matter what.

The Lev Tov writes that if someone trusts in something besides Hashem, Hashem will leave that person alone. The day will come that the person is going to feel stupid for trusting in something other than Hashem, because Hashem is in charge of everything—money, house, everything out there. Hashem is in charge, so have trust in Him and nobody else.

When you trust Hashem, you are blessed and Hashem will trust in you and be with you at all times. Just work on trusting Hashem. Tell yourself. "Whatever is happening, Hashem, I know You are doing it and I love You and I trust You." That is how you build trust with Hashem.

I will conclude with a parable:

A father takes his son to a doctor for a flu shot. They are waiting for the doctor to come in. A few minutes go by and the doctor walks in and says, "Sir, hold your son so I can give him the flu shot."

The son starts to cry and when sees his father is allowing the doctor to give him the shot, he can't believe his eyes. He is crying nonstop and the father tells the son, "This is for your good, son. Don't worry, you're going to be okay."

The parable teaches us a lesson in life: When you face difficulties in life, know in your heart that Hashem loves you, and no matter what He's doing, it's because He cares about you.

Rabbi Avigdor Miller says—and this is something we all should apply it to our lives—People are created in this world not just to avoid sinning but to have achievements and that is accomplished by learning Torah, doing *chesed* for others, and trusting Hashem.

Good things will take you to a good place.

85. We All Have One Father

It states in *Tehillim* that a father always has mercy on his children.

Each person has his own problems, whether it's sickness, Heaven forbid, a livelihood, finding a *shidduch*, learning the Torah the right way.

Everyone has something they have to work on.

If you truly want something, you must turn to Hashem and pray to Him. That is because Hashem has mercy on you more than anyone out there.

Hashem is there to save you and help you with all your problems. One of Hashem's Names is made of a *yud* and a *hei*, which can be used to form two words: *Yad*, which means *hand*, and *hoshi'ah*, which means *save*.

Hashem's hand is always helping you. Hashem is there to save you and protect you and give you what you really need and deserve.

A famous Gemara states that if a man has good deeds and has Torah study in him, then he deserves a wife with the same actions.

Many people want to marry the best people out there—but wait! Look at your actions and ask yourself two simple questions:

1. Are your actions good?
2. Are you going in the direction of Hashem?

Hashem is there to give you what fits for you, because He is the only One Who knows what you truly deserve, whether bad or good.

Hashem has His plans and knows why things happen to people.

We all have one Father, and that is HaKadosh Baruch Hu—Hashem Who is running the world the way He knows it should be.

Hashem is there to do good for everybody, but first you have to do good to yourself. Once you fix your middot, you'll see good in your life. As it states in the *Amidah*, *Sim shalom tovah*, Hashem is there to do good for everyone.

Remember one thing: We only have one Father Who cares about us more than anyone out there, and that is Hashem.

86. Allow Hashem to Fight Your Problems

Every morning during our prayers, in *Baruch She'amar* we say the powerful words, "Blessed are You, Hashem, Who makes decrees and fulfills them."

Whether good and bad comes your way, know that you still bless Hashem for making the decrees, because Hashem knows what's best for you.

If, Heaven forbid, you have a problem, don't allow yourself to suffer trying to fix the issue; rather, allow Hashem to fight your problems.

In the *Amidah* we say these words:

Re'eh nah b'anyeinu, Look, please, upon our affliction, *v'rivei riveinu*, and defend our cause.

We say Hashem, look at our affliction and defend us from them.

Each person who is going through a struggle, Heaven forbid, should always remember that your Father that is giving you the problem.

He wants you to pray to Him and ask Him for help.

Don't allow yourself to fight to fix the issue, but rather call out to Hashem and cry out to Him, because Hashem hears your prayers and He is waiting for you to call out to Him.

Tehillim states, *Hashem shamah*, Hashem hears you.

Never tell yourself, "I can't pray anymore; I keep on praying to Hashem but He is just not listening to my prayers."

In truth, Hashem does hear your prayers and does feel your pain; you must have hope in Hashem and not giving up on your prayers.

Hashem wants to deal with your problem, but when a person, Heaven forbid, starts to blame himself or herself by saying, "It's all caused by me; I made this mistake and I spoke like this, I should've done this…." No! Don't blame yourself; accept what you are going through and pray to Hashem for help.

Hashem is there for everyone—you just have to call out to Him in truth.

One of Hashem's Names is spelled *mem, hei, shin*.

The three letters can represent words:

Mem is for *makom*, place, meaning the place where you are in life, whether it's in learning, school, work, or wherever you are in life.

Hei is for Hashem Himself.

Shin is for *Shomer*; Hashem is watching you with whatever you are going through.

Always remember these three letters of Hashem's Name, which come to teach us that whichever place you are, Hashem watches you and wants to fix your problem.

Just allow him to do so. Stop fooling yourself by it's all through your strength and with your hands that you are doing all these actions.

You always need Hashem in your life because Hashem is the One Who gave you all the great gifts in life.

Hashem wants to fight your problems— but you have to give Him the chance to do so.

87. What Are We Living For?

Each person has to ask himself or herself this simple question:

What am I living for? It sounds like an easy question, but for some people it's hard to answer. WHY? Because majority of the people are so attached to all the *gashmiyut* around them, whether it's money, houses, cars, and all the luxury out there, and that is a big mistake.

Ask yourself: What are you living for? Are you living for living in this world, toiling in Torah and doing good deeds? That is everyone's purpose in living in this world.

What makes you alive is the Torah; the more Torah you learn, the more you are alive. As it states, *Marbeh Torah, marbeh chaim*, the more Torah you learn, the more you are alive.

Sometimes a person says, "I learn Torah, but it's useless. I'm wasting my time; why should I learn?" Each person has an inner negative force in himself or herself that makes them think at times that they are wasting their time in doing good deeds. The simple answer is, it's all the *yetzer hara*!

When you are trying to reach for greatness, that is when the *yetzer hara* tries to attack you, but in truth, that is a test, so you should keep battling the battle and don't stop that till the end. Rabbi Ezra Dayan said that by just battling the *yetzer hara*, you are a winner!

Each person is supposed to be living for one thing, and that is learning the Torah and performing good deeds in this world. All Jewish people have a portion in *Olam Haba*.

It's in your hands to answer that question.
Ask yourself: What am I living for?

88. Return to the Torah

To be alive, each person needs Torah. A person who lives in this world and has no Torah is not living for the truth. To be alive, you need something to strive for, and that is the Torah. Torah is the only thing that makes a person alive. The Mishna in *Avot* states, "The more Torah you learn, the more you are alive." To help understand this concept, it can be compared to a person who is, Heaven forbid, starving and hasn't eaten in days. How do you think he is feeling? He is very weak. The same is true regarding a person who has no Torah: he is spiritually weak!

To make your spirit alive, you have to know what to strive for—and that is the Torah.

The summer days can be really dangerous for each person out there- A person who is enjoying the summer and has no Torah can fall into a trap of the *yetzer hara*! A person needs more Torah in one day of the summer than in all other days combined. Summer days are when a person should learn every day. You want to have a holy summer, not the opposite, *chas v'shalom*.

You all have the ability to return to the Torah. You just have to try it out and make yourself taste the sweetness of Torah.

When you are engaged in Torah study, it's a protection for you that will save you from danger and sins. That is the power of learning the Torah. It's never too late. we have something to prove to us that there's always another chance. In the *Amidah* we say the words, *Hashevenu Avenu l'Toratecha*, Father, return us to Your Torah.

Every day when you are saying these words, you're talking to your Father in Heaven, and you are saying, "Return me to Your Torah."

We all have the great advantage of returning to the Torah; it's all about making that decision.

That is why when a person comes to learn the Torah, he will repent. *Vahzerenu beteshuva*, Return us in repentance. That can happen only when a person is learning the Torah. When you learn, you are wiping away all the sins you committed.

We are placed in this world to toil in Torah (*Mesillat Yesharim*, Chapter 1).

Each person on his or her personal level must ask, "How am I going to make my summer kosher?"

89. The Light of a Person

When a person is engaged in Torah studies, the light of the person gets brighter and brighter.

The more you give up everything for the Torah, you are making a light in you that you, yourself don't even know. When you sit down with a Gemara and try to read the Gemara, they are making a celebration for you in *Shamayim* and you are making your portion in Heaven.

If, *chas v'shalom*, a person is disconnected from the Torah, then he is making that light inside him darker and darker.

People think, "Why do I need Torah in my life? I'm enjoying my life. I'm doing more important things, trying to make money, hanging out, going out, etc." They say they will learn Torah later, when they have time. You fools! That is the evil inclination that makes people feel they are having a blast, but that is very short term, not long term.

A famous Gemara in *Kiddushin* states that Hashem created the *yetzer hara* but He also created something to destroy it, and that is the Torah. Torah is the protection that will protect you from sin and danger.

Torah makes a person light up and it's the solution for everything.

The true light of a person is to toil in the Torah as much as he can.

When a person places himself in an environment that has Torah, he is building himself and his future.

Rabbi Eliezer Ginsberg said once that to build his or her future, a person must make the right decision and if a person will choose Torah learning he or she will have a life full of good! But if, *chas v'shalom*, the other way around, that person's whole life will be full of stupidity and miss the whole point of why he or she is alive.

A well-known halacha states that each man is obligated to learn Torah (*Rambam, Hilchot Limud Torah*). We are obligated to learn Torah day and night.

We all have to try to commit to learn as much as we can, because the only true light that we can get is the Torah.

90. There's No One Like Hashem Who Is Like Hashem?

Every morning we say the words, "There's no one like Hashem."

Each person should have this in his mind every day of his life and train himself that there's no one like Hashem.

Hashem is the One Who placed you in this world, and that itself is the biggest gift. Many times in life, we face little afflictions, and we overhear ourselves thinking that we are in charge. However, in reality and truth, we are not in charge at all.

Hashem is the only One in charge and that is the reason we say these powerful words: There's no one like Hashem.

Short parable helps us understand this concept better.

A son is always going to believe that his father will be there for him and take care of him. If one day a random person walks in the house and tells the child, "I'm your real father," the son will look at this person and say, "No! I only have one Tatte! I have only one father."

The *nimshal* that we can learn in life and always train ourselves to know is that there's only one Father, and that is Hashem.

We have to train our minds to think like that and live it in this world: In truth, there's only one Father. Many people can say the words, "Hashem—I love him and He's in charge," but when things come your way, you still have to be the same person. The way you can do it is by training yourself every day to say the words, to scream the words, *En Od Melavado*.

Who is like our G-d? The answer to that question is: There's no one like our Father.

Hashem is always there for His children and you just have to believe it. The more we work on ourselves by saying these words and placing them in our minds and hearts, the more we will reach the heights of *emuna* and *bitachon*.

The Chatam Sofer writes that to understand that there is Hashem in the world, you have to apply these words to your heart.

There is no one like Hashem.

91. The Fruit of Life

When you go to a farm and you see all the fruits growing so amazingly, you have to recognize that that is the *chesed* of Hashem.

Look at a peach. The first thing you should do is have in mind and tell yourself how amazing Hashem's creation is. By doing that, you are applying the *middah* of having awareness of Hashem. Then say the *beracha* and eat the peach; after that, thank Hashem for the amazing gift you have seen and eaten.

Each Jew is compared to a tree. When you go in the direction of Hashem, you'll see your kids become *talmidei chachamim* and you'll see how powerful it is to perform good deeds in this world.

When you are in this world and perform good deeds and learn Torah, you'll create fruits—those fruits will be the people who will follow Hashem's path.

The question is, what does the fruit of life have to do with us? I will answer this question with a parable so that we can all understand the question and apply the answer to our daily life.

A person goes to a farm and picks a peach and recites the blessing.

He takes a bite and his face lights up and he says, "Wow! This is the best taste I ever tasted in my entire life!"

He keeps on eating that peach and enjoying Hashem's creation and tells himself, "Wow! It's so good! I will never forget this taste."

The Torah we learn and the misvot we do the correct way are compared to the fruit of life. The same way the person ate the peach and enjoyed every second, so too, we have to compare this to our life. Every time you learn Torah and perform misvot, don't forget about them.

Torah and misvot are your life and they are going to make you enter *Olam Haba*.

92. Stay Happy

One of the hardest deeds is remaining happy in this world. We see many things happening in the world that disappoint us. It gets harder to remain in a good mood in a good environment.

We should know an important thing and always remind ourselves that the things that Hashem makes us see are a wake-up call for us to wake up and straighten ourselves to go in Hashem's way.

When a tragedy happens, it's for us to ask ourselves if we're doing the right thing in this world. That is something each person is obligated to do: to check his deeds and see if he's going in the right path. And when we see things that disappoint us, it's because of something that we have to fix in ourselves to become happy. Whatever Hashem does for us is for the best, and we still have to continue performing the service of Hashem.

A parable may help us understand this point better.

The owner of a company wants to hire a salesperson. He interviews a man who is looking for a job, and then tells him, "You'll get salary and commission, based on your sales. You can start next Monday. I'll see you at 9:00 a.m. in my office." "Thank you! Have a great day."

The next week, the salesperson gets to the office on time. He's very happy and asks the owner, "When can I start working? I want to go out and start selling."

The owner says, "If you're confident enough, you can go now."

The salesperson takes a train to a buyer, hoping he will make his first sale and impress his boss. One buyer after another doesn't want to buy anything. All of a sudden, the salesperson becomes very disappointed.

The salesperson is not happy at all. He gets back to the office and tells his boss, "Steve, I don't understand. Why didn't anybody buy from me? I don't know what I did wrong. Can you please help me out?"

The boss asks him a simple question. "When you spoke to the buyers, did you have your happy mood on?"

The salesperson puts his head down and says, "No, I didn't. I was nervous and wasn't happy at all. The reason why I was nervous is because I didn't know what to say."

The boss says, "I will give you one word of advice, and I want you to remember this for your rest of your life. Whatever goes on, you always have to remain happy, and when you talk to buyers, you must be happy and know what to tell them."

The question is, what is this parable trying to hint to us? We all live in a world in which it's very hard to remain happy and do good in this world, but we always have to remind ourselves that no matter what life throws at us we always have to remain happy and do the service of G-d.

Always stay happy because that is what G-d wants from you, not to fall into depression, Heaven forbid.

93. Don't Take Revenge

When a person, *chas v'shalom*, takes revenge on his or her friend, know that the Torah forbids the person to do so.

We see this many times. Jack will ask David for a favor and David says he can't do it. David feels bad because he couldn't help Jack. Even though he didn't do the favor, by just feeling bad about it, it's as if he did it.

If the next day David asks Jack for a favor and Jack says, "No, I'm not going to do you that favor! You didn't do me a favor when I asked you," that is taking revenge. Just because people can't help you when you ask, that doesn't mean you should hold a grudge.

If you are capable of helping your fellow, do it! Don't tell yourself, "But this person never helps me." Don't take revenge.

Negative thoughts that sometimes enter our mind include, "Why should I do it for him if he didn't do it for me?" "Why should I go to his wedding if he didn't come to mine?" And the list goes on.

These thoughts must leave our mindset so we can make ourselves who we really are.

A famous Gemara in *Shabbat* reinforces this lesson.

A convert wanted to learn Torah. He went to Bet Shammai and said, "Teach me the whole Torah on one foot." Bet Shammai told him to get out!

Then the convert went to Bet Hillel and made the same request. Bet Hillel told him, "I will teach you the whole Torah on one condition: that you won't harm others just like you won't harm yourself." This is loving your fellow Jew.

The next time you are asked to do someone a favor, don't refuse and don't hold a grudge or take revenge, because they are all forbidden by the Torah.

94. Don't Be Frustrated

When you are asked to perform a misva or any good thing and you perform it and while your performing with your friend, the plan doesn't work out, don't be frustrated with your friend.

Show gratitude to your friend because he tried to help you with the action but Hashem didn't allow him to be successful. Instead of being frustrated at people and yourself because your plan didn't work, don't be upset. Hashem is running the show.

If one morning you wake up and you want to make a cup of coffee before you go to work and you notice that there isn't milk in the fridge or the milk is spoiled, don't be upset and start complaining. Rather, close your eyes and say, "Hashem, I accept what You did and I am going to drink the coffee without milk." This is the attitude we all have to have—not to be frustrated.

This is the *middah* each person has to work on, not to be upset if something doesn't go your way.

If you think logically, you will realize that there is no point in getting angry if there's no milk. and the answer is that you gain nothing.

That's why you're supposed to be happy and thank Hashem.

When you become frustrated and you're always getting upset, you'll have the *middah* of anger, and the sages tells us that anyone who has anger is like someone worshiping idols.

Why is anger compared to worshiping idols? When a person is angry, that shows he doesn't trust in God and he is hitting walls because he or she is getting frustrated. When you are frustrated, it means that your *emuna* and *bitachon*—your faith and trust in Hashem—are weak.

Once you have strong *emuna* and *bitachon*, you'll never come to be frustrated.

When you have trust in God you have tranquility. Then, no matter what G-d throws at you, you'll remain calm. That is the power of having trust in faith.

Faith is knowing that God is there and trust means that you trust that anything that happens to you, you'll be calm.

95. People Need Chizuk

We live in a world in which everyone needs *chizuk*. A person doing something good always would want *chizuk* for doing it.

When a person sacrifices everything he has in order to learn Torah, be the one to give him *chizuk* by telling him, "Wow! You're so lucky—you get to learn Torah all day!" By giving him *chizuk*, you are uplifting him and encouraging him to want to grow more.

People need *chizuk* to keep on doing good. Without *chizuk*, people would fall in a big pit and they wouldn't want to do good. You may see someone doing a great deed but no one encourages him. How do you think he'll feel? He'll be upset and not want to strive for the truth.

When a person goes up for an *aliyah* on Shabbat day, be the one to greet him by saying, "*Chazak u'barchu*!" That is giving *chizuk*.

Rabbi Eliyahu Dessler, known as the Michtav Me'Eliyahu, asks: How do you bring people to love Torah and become closer to Hashem?

Rabbi Dessler answers, it's by you giving in, being a "Giver." You must be a giver to people by giving them *chizuk*.

When you see a person who is struggling with something in life and you have *bitachon*, don't just say, "Trust in Hashem"; give in and help him out with what's happening to him.

I heard about a student who went to the Chofetz Chaim to ask him a question. The student asked, "What can I do so Hashem will hear my *tefillot*?"

The Chofetz Chaim answered, "By helping others and performing *chesed*. When you help others, Hashem will help you."

Be the one to give people *chizuk*!

96. The Danger of Technology

We live in a world full of technology that is harming our children today. The saddest part is that parents are allowing their children to have access to all the garbage that's out there.

Every other month something new comes out, making our children move further from Hashem and not want to learn the Torah the right way.

Wrongly used technology is destroying us today and we have to avoid harmful devices by not giving them to our kids or to anybody else.

Technology can destroy homes, shidduchim, businesses. We all have to stay away from using technology the wrong way.

97. Cry Out

Tehillim 27:7 states, "Hashem, hear my voice and have favor in me and answer me."

When you cry out to Hashem with *tefillot*, saying, "Hashem, please help me out with the situation I am going through," Hashem will hear your cry. Hashem is there for everyone, and especially for the people with broken hearts. Hashem automatically hears your *tefillot*.

Take upon yourself one *beracha* in the *Amidah* and cry out to Hashem and you'll see results. It's a guarantee, as it states, the only gates that are always open are the Gates of Tears. That is why you should cry out and pray as much as you can. The more you pray, the more you feel accomplished, and the more you feel accomplished the more you feel happy. Cry out to Him today.

98. The Importance of Having a Realization

It is important to have the view in this world that you are making yourself closer to G-d. You should have the realization that this world is the entryway to Heaven and you are looking and searching for what is going to help you get there. Each person should ask, "What are we doing in this world? Are we toiling or are we lacking?"

Start to have your own vision to life and realize the truth of this world is only learning Torah and performing *chesed*.

May we all have a good vision in our lives

99. Cling to Hashem

Parashat Va'ethanan states how powerful it is to become close to Hashem. You'll have a great life and tranquility in this world, because in truth there is nothing greater than being close to the Master of the universe.

The *pasuk* states, "Those who attach themselves to Me will have many days to their lives." When you attach yourself to Hashem, you will know the meaning of life. David HaMelech said that all his life he attached himself to Hashem and always did good.

Many times, in life people face difficulties, whether its earning a living or finding a spouse. If we always keep this concept in mind, we will always remember that Hashem only does what's for our benefit.

The *pasuk* writes in *Va'ethanan*, that we should watch the misvot and perform them. When a person learns Torah and performs misvot, he is attaching himself to Hashem.

These powerful words tell us that we must watch the misvot and do them. A person who does work *l'shem Shamayim* is attaching himself to Hashem.

When it says to watch the misvot, it means to say, "Look, My child, look at this misva. If you do this misva, you'll get close to Me."

Once you do them, you will be closer to Him.

When a person does good deeds in this world, he will come to love Hashem; as it states in the first paragraph of *Shema*, "You should love Hashem your G-d." To love Hashem means that you are READY to do anything for Him, no matter what.

Our job in this world is to do what Hashem commanded us and to be close to Him as possible.

100. Perform Misvot in This World

It states, "Cause me to walk on the path of Your misvot." Each person must have this in mind: In this world, it's not about running after every garbage out there, but rather to run after every misva that comes your way. The misvot that people do in this world will help them enter into *Olam Haba*. Without misvot you cannot get in. A parable will help us understand this better.

A person wants to fly to Israel, so he goes to the airport and he says, "I want to fly."

They ask him, "Sir, where's your ticket?" He replies, "I have a passport."

They say, "No, sir, a passport isn't enough. You also need to buy a ticket."

This parable comes to teach us that to enter *Olam Haba*, you must have a ticket, and your ticket is your misvot.

Every time a person does misvot, they are lighting themselves with the true light of life, and that true light is going to make them enter *Olam Haba*. Misvot are what protect a person; without misvot you are putting yourself in danger. Every misva you do is a protection for you and your house hold. That is the privilege of performing misvot.

When you commit a sin, Heaven forbid, you are putting yourself in danger and you are letting the *Shechina* disappear from you. We don't want that, we want the *Shechina* to be with us always.

Many people seek help. They go to every rabbi they can find for help, and the rabbis try to help them but the people don't help themselves and that is a very big mistake. People who want to have a good home must ask themselves, "Am I doing what Hashem wants me to do or I am doing the opposite?"

Hashem wants everyone back, no matter how bad they were. He loves you and will always do for you, but you must control yourself by staying away from sinning. The more you stay away from sinning, the more you'll see blessing in your life.

Rabbi Avigdor Miller says that when doing a misva, you have to do it with the intention that you love to perform misvot; that is the right attitude.

The misvot that a person does in this world are his or her ticket to enter *Olam Haba*.

You can't fly to Israel without buying a ticket; so too, you can't enter *Olam Haba* without doing misvot.

Biography

My parents immigrated from Syria in 1991, and I was born 1996 in the Brooklyn, New York, the youngest of three sons. My parents sent me to learn in Yeshivat Ohr HaTorah, where I was very inspired to learn and to grow spiritually and in my Torah studies. I was greatly helped and inspired by my wonderful mentor, Rabbi Yaakov Kalmanowitz, who encouraged me to improve my *middot* and become a true *ben Torah*.

AGer high school, at the age of seventeen, I was fortunate to go to Israel to learn in Yeshivat Lev Aharon to learn Torah and to become a better person. I sat down and learned how to become a better person and how to serve Hashem the right way. Each night, aGer learning *seder*, I would go into the *beit midrash* and write my thoughts about what we had learned and how the learning can be applied to my own life and to the lives of others. I became inspired to compose short essays how a person should behave and how he can serve Hashem better. Those essays are the foundation of this volume. The bases of my writing are from *Tehillim*, *Mishlei*, Gemara, and Chumash.

In 2013 when I returned from Israel, I started learning in Yeshivat Yad Yosef, Rabbi David Ashear is my Rebbe who is still teaching me the guidelines of *emuna* and *bitachon*. May Hashem Bless Him. Amen.

I recently married my wonderful *kallah*, Bella Yaich. and we are hoping to build a *bayit ne'eman b'Yisrael*.

I want to help others to realize their *tachlit* in life, to realize the purpose of living, and to set goals for themselves that will help them achieve happiness by becoming close to Hashem Yitbarach. This book is meant to help people do the right things and have an open vision to life.

I was inspired to write everything down because I love to give people encouragement to do good. This book is meant to help people in their everyday lives.

I hope *b'ezrat Hashem* to continue to learn and to help others come to the realization that the *Bore Olam* is waiting for us to come close to Him so that He can bring *Mashiach* soon. Amen.

I was greatly helped and inspired by my wonderful mentors Rabbi Yaakov Kalmanowitz and Rabbi David Ashear, who are still encouraging me to improve my character and become a true person. G-d gave me the ability to write short essays on how a person should behave and on how a person can serve God better.

Those essays are the foundation of the second volume of *The Vision of Life*. The sources in my writing are mainly from Gemara, Chumash, *Tehillim*, and *Mishlei*.

Both books are meant to help people realize the truth of living in this world. Each topic will help a person go in G-d's way and become a great Jew.

I hope with G-d's help to always grow in G-d's way.

www.ingramcontent.com/pod-product-compliance
Lightning Source LLC
Chambersburg PA
CBHW052210090526
44584CB00016BA/2077